T0247861

MARRIED...
WITH CHILDREN
vs. THE WORLD

The INSIDE STORY of
the SHOCK-COM that LAUNCHED FOX
and CHANGED TV COMEDY FOREVER

RICHARD GURMAN

PERMUTED
PRESS

A PERMUTED PRESS BOOK
ISBN: 978-1-63758-831-4
ISBN (eBook): 978-1-63758-832-1

Married… With Children vs the World:
The Inside Story of the Shock-Com that Launched FOX and
Changed TV Comedy Forever
© 2024 by Richard Gurman
All Rights Reserved

"Married… with Children" © 1987, 2022
ELP Communication Inc.
All images courtesy of Sony Pictures Television

Cover design by Conroy Accord

PERMUTED
PRESS

Permuted Press, LLC
New York • Nashville
permutedpress.com

Published in the United States of America
1 2 3 4 5 6 7 8 9 10

I would like to dedicate this book to Ron Leavitt
and Michael Moye without whose courage,
vision and groundbreaking sense of humor
this series could never have been written.

I would like to acknowledge my loving wife, Susan
Gurman, without whose encouragement, patience
and insight this book could never have been written.

And I would also like to acknowledge the tremendous
creative contributions of my editor, Jacob Hoye,
and my agent Simon Green, whose unselfish
collaboration helped me achieve a very different
type of writing than I have ever attempted.

CONTENTS

PREFACE

On April 5, 1987, at 7:00 PM eastern time, *Married... With Children* aired its first episode on the new FOX Network with Ronald Reagan in the White House, yuppie culture peaking, gas prices at eighty-nine cents per gallon, Lady Gaga one year old, and *The Cosby Show, Family Ties,* and *Growing Pains* atop the TV rankings. By 1990, after a slow start and a moral crusade that almost got the series cancelled, *Married... With Children* became FOX TV's first breakout hit, scoring especially high in the eighteen-to-thirty-four-year-old youth demographic that advertisers covet. By 1997, after eleven seasons on the air, the controversial show became the longest-running scripted series in FOX Network history and the second-longest-running sitcom in all TV history, with 263 episodes—just one below *Frasier* (264), outranking such all-time hits as *Friends* (239) *Cosby* (201), and *Seinfeld* (180).

Impressive as these statistics are, they only hint at conveying *Married... With Children*'s enduring impact on our popular culture. A recent article in *New York Magazine* called it, "one of the most influential shows ever made," and ranked it fifth in a survey of "The 50 Most Definitive Series of All Time." As Peter Roth, former president of FOX and Warner Brothers Television, put it: "It's fair to say that there would be no *Married... With Children* without FOX and no FOX, as we know it, without *Married... With Children.*"

What started simply as a crude parody of traditional network sitcoms, *Married* pushed the boundaries of acceptable language and subject matter on network TV, presenting a more realistic, biting picture of family life, ironically ending up as a blueprint for the very establishment it mocked, as evidenced by the many shows that followed down its wayward path: *Roseanne, Everybody Loves Raymond, Arrested Development, It's Always Sunny in Philadelphia, Family Guy, Modern Family, Schitt's Creek*, and many more. And there is no end in sight, as *Married... With Children* reruns are still in heavy rotation on many cable stations and streaming services, with an animated *Married... With Children* series, featuring the voices of the original cast, in the works.

Married... With Children's lasting influence on the culture is further marked by how many subsequent hit shows in which its cast members starred, guest-starred or hosted: *Modern Family, Sons of Anarchy, Friends, The West Wing, 8 Simple Rules, The Big Bang Theory, Saturday Night Live, So You Think You Can Dance, Futurama, Dead to Me*, and *The Conners*, to name a few.

Most of all, *Married... With Children*'s legacy must be viewed in the context of being a cutting-edge show, portraying marriage unlike any other family TV comedy that preceded it, debuting with no recognizable stars on a totally unknown network with limited audience coverage in an era when a staunch conservative president was elected by a landslide. As media analyst Steve Lablang noted: "Not since Milton Berle's *Texaco Star Theatre* put NBC on the map at the dawn of television, has any one show had such an impact on a network and the TV landscape as *Married... With Children*."

Unsurprisingly, the inner workings and behind-the-scenes adventures of this unabashedly irreverent show were just as tumultuous and uproarious as the series itself. This secret layer was a high-stakes game of Whack-A-Mole with breakout stars, media moguls, comedic geniuses, LGBTQ+ activists, pro wrestlers, a teen siren, Playboy Playmates, hip-hop artists, moral crusaders, and anxious sponsors. Most of these shared the same passion for success, but had very different, often conflicting ideas of how to achieve it. But achieve it they did and, in most cases, parlayed that success into career and financial highs that are still on the rise.

I was lucky enough to be a writer/producer on *Married... With Children* from its rocky beginning, where we were fighting the network to get our show on the air every week, to the bittersweet end, where we were fighting *each other* to get our show on the air every week. It is my passion and privilege to share the behind (and in front of) the scenes spectacle with you in this book. But you don't have to just take my word for it. Along with my own memories of the show, I've drawn on firsthand accounts of many of the actors, writers, network executives, journalists, ardent fans, and offended detractors who were either buckled into or trying to derail this wild ride. Having relived many of the unapologetically crude and surprisingly touching moments from classic episodes and offstage moments that were as funny and over the top as the series itself, I enjoy sharing them with you. The show may have been cancelled, but *Married... With Children* lives on in syndication, streaming services, podcasts, blogs, YouTube (172,000 *Married* subscribers), TikTok (576.9 million *Married* views) and other social media highlight compilations, cultural references, foreign remakes, fans' memories, and the pages that follow.

In the final episode of the first season of *Married... With Children*, Al Bundy, forced to stay home and solve his family's incessant domestic problems instead of going out to enjoy a rowdy celebration with his friends, shoots a question to the heavens that reflects not only his predicament in the moment, but his lot in life and the central query of this book:

> **AL:** Never wanted to get married—I'm married. Never wanted to have kids—I got two of 'em. How the hell did this happen?

How the hell did *Married... With Children* happen? Let's find out.

CHAPTER 1

INTRODUCTION: THE BIRTH OF A NETWORK... AND A SERIES

ON APRIL 5, 1987, THE FOX Broadcasting Company (commonly known as FOX) launched the first new American television network in over forty years, with the pilot episode of *Married... With Children* and surprisingly little fanfare. The *New York Times* called it, simply: "The premier of a half-hour comedy about a suburban couple with two teenage children," but there was nothing really simple about it. Its creation required an unholy alliance between an ultraconservative media mogul and a team of two brilliant, scruffy, irreverent, balls-to-the-wall comedy writers that could only have been accomplished by a concerted effort to put each of their considerable differences aside, give a collective middle finger to traditional network programming, and hope to emerge successful from the shitstorm that was sure to follow. As *Married... With Children* series cocreator Michael Moye told me, "It was like trying to launch a luxury liner by breaking a bottle of Boone's Farm over the bow."

For almost six decades prior to FOX's network debut, the TV business had been monopolized by the so-called Big Three:

ABC, CBS and NBC. FOX's gambit to join their established ranks was a long shot at best. Just to have a seat at the network table, publisher Rupert Murdoch had to ante up $250 million for 20th Century Fox Studios, knowing he would have to spend billions more to acquire enough independent TV stations and broadcast groups to even have a shot at competing in their high stakes game. On top of that, he had the even more daunting task of creating a plan to break the iron grip on the nation's viewers ABC, NBC, and CBS held for so many decades and convince advertisers that FOX could provide the kind of programming that would reverse those entrenched viewing patterns.

FOX's principal strategy was to create shows so bold, controversial, and flat-out different from the traditional networks that viewers would, at the very least, be shocked into watching. Barry Diller, FOX's CEO and Murdoch's architect in this scheme, made this clear to his staff when he told them: "Unless you grab the audience by the neck, by the shirt collar and drag them to this other channel, they're not coming."

But it wasn't just any viewer the nascent network was trying to shock into watching. According to Rick DuBrow, writing in the *Los Angeles Times* at the time: "What FOX is really doing is much more significant, like it or not. Frankly, targeting the young audience, it is more blatantly, irreverently—and often more honestly—trying to reflect the outlooks of this age group than any other network except ABC."

Ted Harbert, ABC's president during this startup period, however, told me: "I didn't take the FOX threat very seriously, but I knew Barry Diller was really smart. I was just glad I wasn't working for that screamer."

Michael Fuchs, who was chairman of rival HBO at the time, said he is convinced there is at least one baby picture of Diller "with a cigar in his mouth and a gavel in his hand."

To fathom just how much of a sea change FOX's disruptive strategy represented in the highly corporate, profit-driven world of network television, it's important to note that from TV's first commercial in 1941 (a ten-second spot for Bulova watches) to the late 1980s when FOX was launched, every network's Golden Rule was *Thou Shalt Not Offend Anyone, Lest They Turn the Channel.* For example, in the 1950s, when Lucy was pregnant on *I Love Lucy*, CBS feared that even saying the word "pregnant" would turn viewers off, so they referred to her as "expecting," or "with child." Sexual lines were also narrowly drawn in the '60s on *Gilligan's Island, Gidget,* and *I Dream of Jeannie*, where the lead women were barred from wearing wardrobe that showed their navels...though NBC didn't seem to mind Jeannie referring to her boyfriend on the series as "Master."

On the mid-'70s sitcom *Happy Days*, ABC feared Fonzie's signature leather motorcycle jacket made him look like a "criminal" and wanted him to stop wearing it. Series creator/producer Garry Marshall, however, claimed Fonzie was doing ABC's audience a public service by wearing leather, as it protects bikers from injury in case they fell. ABC *fell* for Garry's story: *Happy Days* went on to become the number-one show on TV and Fonzie's jacket went on display in the Smithsonian National Museum of American History.

FOX, aware of these conservative guardrails, and knowing it needed to lure the most successful, generally free-spirited writers to their lower-paying startup venture, made a bargain with them—if they created shows for FOX, they were guaranteed the creative freedom they could never get at the Big Three. This persuaded some of the top writers in Hollywood to create the type of distinctive programing FOX was counting on. For example, Stephen Cannell's teen cop drama, *21 Jump Street*, starring Johnny Depp; James L. Brooks' sketch comedy series, *The Tracey Ullman Show*, starring Tracey Ullman; Ed. Weinberger's *Mr. President*, starring George C. Scott; and Ron Leavitt and Michael Moye's antisitcom, *Married... With Children*, starring no one...yet.

Then, to prove FOX was putting its money where its potty mouth was, it scheduled the hard-edged, raunchy *Married... With Children*, as the first series of this entire lineup to launch its network. Though it struggled mightily in the ratings at first, in the long run, this turned out to be a good bet. FOX and its raunchy series eventually caught on to the extent that, in 1996, *Married... With Children* became the longest-running live action TV series on the air, and in 2019, Disney bought FOX from Rupert Murdoch for 71.3 billion dollars...not a bad return on his $250 million.

Looking back at FOX's disruptive strategy and the shows it spawned, the question some observers have raised is, was the new network really a champion of creative freedom, or was it just a cynical ploy to cash in on the changes already afoot in the culture and the TV audience that the entrenched, Big Three networks were too slow to respond to by themselves? "The corporate bosses at the Big Three at the time," Ted Harbert pointed out, "were older white guys who didn't want to touch the formula that had made them so much money. The FOX execs (who were *younger* white guys) turned the model on its head."

However, Daniel M. Kimmel in his book, *The Fourth Network*, questions the *creative freedom* aspect of the formula as he points out that: "Diller, time and again, didn't personally like the shows that were putting FOX on the map. He was embarrassed that *Married... With Children* had become the program most closely associated with his network."

While Diller may have set the tone in the FOX executive suites, from what I observed in the trenches back then and in writing this book today, loosening the creative reins was not simply a cynical ploy. Yes, profits were a main target. Why wouldn't they be? More often than not, however, there were key players on *both* sides who still found ways to support and guide the groundbreaking show through the inevitable conflicts that occur with any merger of art and commerce, especially one of this size and provocative intent.

Certainly there were bitter struggles and ugly betrayals along the way, but it was a thrill ride that is in many ways still running, and regardless of the fact that it made a ton of money—as intended—as *also* intended, it broke the mold of the network universe and gave audiences a truly different choice. Or, as the headline of Robert Laurence's review of *Married... With Children*, in the *San Diego Union* so aptly stated:

> "FOX Unleashes New Concept in Television: Comedy That's Funny."

The key player in the cast of this gambit for FOX was Rupert Murdoch, who, before buying FOX Studios, was best known as a tabloid publisher who favored salacious headlines in his *New York Post*, like: "Headless Body in Topless Bar," and (re: the discovery of U.S. Representative Anthony Weiner's dick pics): "Weiner Exposed." However, as Alex Ben Block points out in his book, *Out Foxed*, "Those who were sure he represented the lowest, basest instinct in man, all misunderstood the one lesson that cut across all of Murdoch's media empire was, that good content, good programming and the right popular product could open all kinds of doors." In reality, it knocked them off their hinges.

Next on the credit roll was FOX chairman Barry Diller, the autocratic, powerful CEO who left his job at Paramount Studios to bring his dream of building a fourth TV network to FOX. A cultured man whose TV legacy and taste, including developing the "Movie of the Week," the award winning miniseries *Roots* and the TV series *Cheers*, stood in stark contrast to the sensibilities of *Married... With Children*. While Diller was known to be offended by the series, and was often a huge obstacle to its progress, he also had the guts to put it on the air in the first place, as per his maxim—"To the risk-taker, as always, come the spoils." The ringtone on his cell phone, by the way, is a dog barking.

Jamie Kellner left his lucrative job as CEO of Orion Entertainment to become the first executive hired by Murdoch and Diller as president of FOX, where he was charged with building the affiliate network, selling programming to advertisers, and establishing relations with program producers. According to the *Los Angeles Times*: "Though Barry Diller was practically deified as a visionary for building FOX into a legitimate television network, within the industry it was known that FOX's success had much to do with the low-key Kellner."

Then there was Garth Ancier, NBC's twenty-eight-year-old wunderkind who, over the dire warnings of his bosses there, traded his bright future at the top-rated Peacock Network to join the fledgling FOX as head of programming. "I was twenty-eight years old," Garth told me, "and there's probably no other time in my life when I'd have the bravery and/or stupidity. Why not? I'll work with all these amazing people in all these amazing ventures and whether it succeeds or fails, it's an enormous learning opportunity." Garth was a visionary, a true friend of the show and was single-handedly responsible for convincing Ron Leavitt and Michael Moye to create *Married... With Children* for FOX.

Leavitt and Moye, having built their stellar reputation on traditional sitcoms like *The Jeffersons* and *Silver Spoons* were, nonetheless, dyed-in-the-wool iconoclasts and jumped at the chance to create a show that stoked, what Ron Leavitt described as his, "adolescent rebellion against all those shows where everyone sat together at the dinner table and got along and talked and hugged and solved the world's problems in twenty-two minutes. I would go nuts seeing that."

And, of course, our original cast, Ed O'Neill, Katey Sagal, Christina Applegate, David Faustino, Amanda Bearse and David Garrison, largely unknown actors who by choosing to portray these extremely irreverent characters that the audience would forever identify with them, gambled with their future viability to be cast in more mainstream roles—a bet they stood to lose even more on in success, where the character associations would become indelible. These bold and talented actors turned out to be a mix of very distinct personalities who could enjoy raucous fun offstage yet, at other times, clash as bitterly and openly as their fictional counterparts.

Then there was our *real-world* antagonist, Terry Rakolta, the Michigan woman who launched a highly publicized moral crusade against *Married... With Children* that succeeded not only in getting corporate giants like Proctor & Gamble and Coca-Cola to pull their advertising, which could easily have resulted in FOX cancelling the show, but also, ironically, drove so many new viewers to the brash comedy that it helped save the series and the struggling new FOX Network.

Finally, there was me. Though I couldn't possibly compare myself to the marquee players above, I was fortunate enough to be one of the few people in the delivery room when the Bundy bastard was born. I stuck around to the bittersweet end when we were abruptly and unceremoniously buried in an unmarked grave, which I am here to fittingly mark in the pages of this book.

You see, back then I was a comedy writer, lucky enough to have worked on some of the most memorable sitcoms in TV history—*Happy Days, Laverne & Shirley,* and *Mork & Mindy*. My streak ran out, though, when I became executive producer of the mawkish NBC hit, *The Facts of Life* (a soft comedy about four girls living in a boarding school) and soon found myself embroiled in a battle with the cast over the premise of a script we were shooting where Blair's (one of the main character's) father was arrested in an insider stock-trading scandal.

The actors, taking a network approach, felt that this storyline forever ruined Blair's character, and demanded a total rewrite of the script. I stubbornly, perhaps naively, refused, which led to such a contentious standoff that Glenn Padnick, the president of the studio that produced the show, had to arbitrate. Much to my surprise, he sided with me, forcing the show's long-established stars to perform the script as written by its new executive producer. Even in victory, however, the clash was unnerving. It foreshadowed a bumpy road ahead for me on a series I didn't love, so I took the opportunity to resign. But quitter's remorse soon set in. I had a wife, two kids, a mortgage, and no immediate prospects for another job. *The Facts of Life*, indeed.

As a side note, shortly after my departure, *The Facts of Life* cast convinced NBC to reshoot the episode, this time with Blair's father not only *innocent* of the charge of insider trading, but a *hero* for trying to take the rap for his aging father who had committed the crime because he was feeling powerless and wanted to *get back in the game*. As another side note, George Clooney played a recurring character, the school's handyman, George Burnett, in *The Facts of Life* but he wasn't in this particular episode.

A few weeks after I left *Facts*, sitcom writers Ron Leavitt and Michael Moye handed me a script they had just written for a series for the new FOX network and asked me to consider a job on their show as a writer/producer. I had worked with Ron before and loved his strong work ethic and subversive sense of humor. All I knew of Michael was that he was one of the few African American TV showrunners working at the time and that he shared Ron's penchant for an I-don't-give-a-fuck-how-grungy-I-look wardrobe. One day they showed up at FOX Studios for a meeting with Barry Diller looking so unkempt that the guard at the front gate didn't believe they were there to see the powerful CEO and sent them to the back gate, assuming they were delivery men.

I was desperate for a job at the time, fascinated by how different this show was from the one I had just left and just how much this script had riding on it. So, with a huge rooting interest, I opened the script to the first stage direction and the very first dialogue exchange between Al and Peggy Bundy.

PEGGY SITS ON THE COUCH. AL ENTERS HOLDING A SMALL, POTTED CACTUS PLANT.

AL: Sweetie, is this your little cactus?

PEGGY: Uh-huh.

AL: Any particular reason you put it where the alarm clock used to be?

PEGGY: I thought it would dress up the room a little bit. Oh gee, you know, I meant to tell you to be careful before you slammed your hand down on the alarm this morning.

AL: (HOLDING UP HIS BLOODSTAINED, BANDAGED HAND) Well, you didn't!

PEGGY: Sorry.

AL: It's okay; I stopped the bleeding with your slip.

I'm thinking, *Before Sitcom Mom even says, "Good morning, honey," she has at best carelessly, but quite possibly maliciously, inflicted a bloody wound on Sitcom Dad! This is different. What's next?*

AL OPENS THE REFRIGERATOR AND LOOKS INSIDE.

AL: There's no food.

PEGGY: I didn't have time to shop.

AL: Well, that happens, I understand. You don't have a job or anything, do you?

PEGGY: Well, I do sandpaper the stains out of your shirts and battle your socks and underwear into the washing machine but I guess that is more of an adventure than a job.

Definitely malicious. I'm loving this—Peg can give as well as she gets—but is Barry Diller, the erudite TV pioneer who put Roots *on the air going to approve this crass script to launch his new network? Intrigued, I read on.*

AL: I'm sorry…Anything I can do to make your life a little easier?

PEGGY: You could shave your back.

AL: Hey, that hair's there for a reason. It keeps you offa' me at night.

Okay, this is really funny and, as advertised, totally different. At this point, however, I'm wondering, Where is the magic glue that holds classic TV couples together; the Sam and Diane, Mork and Mindy, Ralph and Alice factor? Do the Bundys have the essential element that makes viewers root for characters, even boorish ones like them, and invite them back into their living room week after week to watch? Then, as if Al and Peg had read my mind, in their own Bundy way, they answered my question.

PEGGY: (LOVINGLY) Al, let's not start. We were having such a nice morning.

AL: (SWEETLY) Yeah, I'm sorry; you're right.

As Al and Peggy slyly smile and perversely-yet-lovingly-connect, they are telling the audience that it's okay to enjoy and laugh with them, because regardless of their harsh tone, neither of them feels at all threatened by the other. They love each other anyway, in a manner that Leavitt and Moye believe millions of couples do too, but that no other show on the air was honest or risky enough to give voice to. Certainly not the Keatons or the Huxtables. In fact, *Married... With Children*'s working title was *We're* Not *the Cosbys*.

Then, in the final scene, to further drive this *twisted-yet-relatable-love* theme home, the Bundys stop their own backstabbing long enough to team up against their smug, newlywed, yuppie neighbors, who have dropped over for their first of what promises to be countless visits, and bait them into what promises to be countless fights of their own. This sends the heretofore lovey-dovey Steve and Marcy squabbling out the door, yelling at each other, as a now-united Al and Peg do a victory dance and go upstairs to have sex.

Let me think: A rude but loving family. A kick in the groin to social status. A hilarious fuck you to every other network sitcom. I'm out of a job. "Hell yes, I'll work on your show. I just pray FOX lets you do it..." Which, as you're about to find out, they almost didn't.

CHAPTER 2

CASTING THE SERIES: WHEN YOU WISH UPON A STAR...SHIT HAPPENS

IMAGINE *MARRIED... WITH CHILDREN* STARRING Sam Kinison and Roseanne Barr instead of Ed O'Neill and Katey Sagal. Or aspiring young actors Tina Caspary and Hunter Carson instead of Christina Applegate and David Faustino. This came perilously close to happening and triggered a bloody, almost fatal, battle between the network and the show before it was even shot.

Whether you consider *Married... With Children* brilliant, vulgar, or, as bestselling novelist Walter Mosley dubbed it: "... brilliantly vulgar," it was clear that casting actors who could play outlandish characters and still be likable to a fresh audience was going to be absolutely essential and especially difficult. "Casting is just one of those things that's so damn hard, especially with comedy," according to Garth Ancier. "You can tank the entire show if you cast badly, and the opposite too. Casting can elevate your material."

Working in our favor to attract good actors, however, was FOX's thirteen episode, on-the-air guarantee. This was a key incentive, as, traditionally, networks ordered up to seventy pilot scripts per year from the TV studios. From these seventy scripts, the networks picked roughly twenty pilots for the studios to shoot, from which the networks chose only five to ten to pick up as series and go on the air. Even in a business accustomed to taking big risks, these were very discouraging odds for a studio or an actor, sustained only by the potentially enormous economic upsides of having a hit show.

Since the upstart FOX couldn't pay studios and writers as much for their product, or guarantee them anywhere near the audience the established networks could, in addition to creative freedom, they lured them with the holy grail of the TV business at that time. Essentially, your project didn't have to compete with the seventy-odd aforementioned pilots being ordered for a handful of time slots on the fall schedule—you were guaranteed from the start to go on the air, at least thirteen times…or, so we thought.

This on-the-air commitment was also powerful bait to snag A-list actors, as being in pilots, which mostly don't make it to series, can be a slow death for performers. As Johnny Carson famously joked on *The Tonight Show* about his fellow comic, Don Rickles: "Don's been in more pilots than an Air Force proctologist." Surprisingly, even with FOX's enticing incentive, casting the perfect Al turned out to be a vexing task, one that would lead to a major pissing contest between our studio and the powerful Barry Diller—the first of many.

The trouble started when our studio, Embassy, thought they could outsmart everyone and bypass the traditional casting/auditioning process by simply making direct series offers to Roseanne Barr and Sam Kinison to play Peggy and Al. It's not uncommon for a studio or a network to build a show around an established star and, thus, capture their built-in fan base: George Lopez, Ellen DeGeneres, and Tina Fey to name a few. It doesn't always work—Dwayne Johnson, Rebel Wilson, and Michael J. Fox all bombed in various shows—but it's a seemingly stable idea in an otherwise shaky world. It also allows executives to deflect any blame if the show fails—"Michael J. Fox was a superstar in *Family Ties*, who knew he would bomb in *The Michael J. Fox Show*? It's not like people didn't know the popular, young star was going to be in it."

In the late '80s, Sam and Roseanne were two of the hottest comics in Hollywood. She had just won the American Comedy Award for Best Female Performer and he was in demand after his hit HBO standup comedy special, *Sam Kinison: Breaking the Rules* and his breakout role in the Rodney Dangerfield film, *Back to School*. Leavitt and Moye had always mentioned Sam and Roseanne as prototypes for Al and Peggy, so it seemed logical to the studio to make them offers to play the parts.

The rub was that Leavitt and Moye had only invoked their names as a shorthand for pitching the show to executives, what's known in the business as an "elevator pitch": "Imagine if Roseanne Barr married Sam Kinison and they had kids." Michael and Ron never intended these comics as the *for-real* cast and were shocked and chagrined to hear the studio had offered them the parts without consulting them.

"We never liked working with comedians," Moye told me, "because they come in with their character already. What were we going to do, tell Roseanne how to do her 'Domestic Goddess' thing? We were gonna tell Sam Kinison how to do his thing? There'd be fighting all the time."

As it turned out, Roseanne and Sam passed on the offers, but the damage was already done. FOX, enticed by the prospect of harnessing these actors' star power to promote its unknown network, was disappointed to lose them. Now, in addition to finding the right actors for these difficult parts, we were challenged to find an Al and Peggy who would also make FOX forget about losing Sam and Roseanne. The truth is, it never actually had them, but in the people at FOX's minds, they would have been perfect. Years later, Kinison would appear as a guest star and leave an unforgettable impression on the show and everyone in it, one that would only serve to made a stronger case for why he should *not* have been cast.

In the meantime, our casting director Marc Hirschfeld immediately started an exhaustive process of auditioning actors for Al Bundy. Marc told me, "Michael Richards came in to read. He was just odd. It was just a very odd read," though Hirschfeld would later cast the *odd Richards* as Kramer in *Seinfeld*. "The challenge was that the material was bigger than life and most of these actors came in and played it extremely broad."

"We saw comic actors," Moye recalls. "We saw Western actors of yesteryear. We saw B- and C-movie stars. Eighty percent of the actors who read for Al played it like Ralph Kramden in *The Honeymooners.* The other twenty percent read it like Jack Nicholson in *The Shining*."

Running out of time—and actors in Hollywood—Hirschfeld asked the producers to see Ed O'Neill, a relatively unknown actor who had impressed Marc in a production of *Of Mice and Men* in Connecticut. "Who the hell is Ed O'Neill?" Moye snapped. "So, he's a dramatic actor? You got any animated actors? You got Yosemite Sam? Sure. Bring him in."

Ed O'Neill, in turn, got a call from his agents, who told him that *Married... With Children* wanted to audition him right away, but his representatives were (as were most agents in Hollywood at the time) very negative about our project—they said it was a horrible show on a dubious new network. "Then what the fuck are you sending me over there for?" Ed inquired. In lieu of an immediate answer, they messengered a copy of the script to the Hollywood YMCA where Ed was playing handball to let him decide for himself.

"I read it and I thought, this is kinda funny," O'Neill told me. "Then I went over to Leavitt and Moye's office and I had my gym bag with all my gloves hanging off it. When you play handball and its warm, you usually sweat through about ten pairs of gloves. So you hang them outside your bag to dry. The minute I came in, Ron and Michael said: 'What the hell is that?' So, I had to explain it to them. And you know what their office looked like, with dartboards and misarranged toys and Ding-Dongs and they were chain-smoking and I thought, *these guys look like gas station attendants*. They asked me if I would read the scene, and I told them, 'Sure, I just read the pilot and, honestly, I think it's funny.'"

Dubious as Leavitt and Moye were about O'Neill before they met him (and even more so after the sweaty gloves deal), what Moye remembers most from the literally hundreds of casting sessions for the Al character, was a chill he felt when, before O'Neill even spoke a single line of dialogue: "He simply opened the (imaginary) door, closed his eyes and let out a world-weary sigh. As far as I was concerned, he didn't have to say another word. That was Al Bundy. Because only Al Bundy would know that no matter what day it was, when he opened that door there was going to be crap on the other side of that door."

Ed told me his own theory on how he got the part. "Sometimes the good fortune is that you don't have the time to get paralysis from analysis. You just pick something quick and go with it. The Bundy character reminded me of an uncle that I have, who was a judge. He was more or less expecting the worst and being okay with it—'Ah Peg, what's for dinner?' 'Oh, Al, I ran over the dog in the driveway; he's dead.' 'Yeah,' Al said, 'but what's for dinner?' That's how I read it and Michael and Ron looked at each other like, 'What the fuck,' because nobody else read it that way."

Finding a candidate for Peggy Bundy turned out to be much easier. Katey Sagal, a former backup singer for Bette Midler and Bob Dylan, impressed everyone with her fresh, assertive take on the character. When she first read the script, however, she recalls envisioning it differently than how it was written: "I had vanity about it because the original script was written that she was slothlike…she was the lazy housewife who laid around eating bonbons. My take was, I did not want to come in in sweats. I kinda put my hair up, and I wore these cat-eyed glasses, a tight dress, and a belt. I thought she should sort of have a retro vibe. I saw her as someone who really cares about herself. She dresses herself up. She's an ex cocktail waitress. I loved that." So did we.

Katey's audition *look* and the sassy attitude that came with it were spot-on and most of it was eventually incorporated into the part. Marc Hirschfeld noted, "The way she carried herself was as if she didn't realize that she was so low class. That to me was the part of Peggy Bundy that she created that was the most fun."

What really surprised me, though, was when Katey told me that the inspiration for her signature "walk," where she shuffles sexily across the room in a way that, in a bygone era, would be described as, "strutting her stuff," had *nothing* to do with how she divined Peggy's essence. It was simply a function of the stacked-heel mule shoes she chose to wear with her tight Capri pants. "Anyone who wears those kind of shoes, you walk a certain way. It was definitely the shoes."

"You know what else I thought," Katey added, "it hadn't been long since I was in a rock band, so I thought, I'm going to disguise this character, so that when I go back to my real job, which is playing music, I won't be mistaken for this person. It kinda worked. I remember doing little promotional things with Eddie, once we were successful and walking down the street. I could go completely unrecognized, but Ed would be swarmed by fans."

Katey had another quality we were desperately looking for. We firmly believed, many decades removed from today's political climate, that you had to create a balance of power in a marriage by writing for and casting a female lead who was as strong, assertive, and funny as our male lead. If she comes off weak, no matter how satirical your intent, you'll cringe rather than laugh at the humor. With Katey's fiery, vain, independent, cocky take on Peggy, the audience never felt she was weak or threatened in any way. If anything, at times, you were concerned for Al.

David Garrison, an accomplished theater actor, who costarred with Jason Bateman in a previous Leavitt and Moye series on NBC, *It's Your Move*, was already approved to play yuppie neighbor Steve Rhoades. Amanda Bearse, who starred in the horror film, *Fright Night*, and actress Rita Wilson were competing to play Steve's banker wife, Marcy.

The leading contenders for Kelly and Bud were two very likable kid actors, Tina Caspary and Hunter Carson (son of Karen Black and Kit Carson). Christina Applegate, who would one day make Kelly Bundy a household name, was not even on our radar, nor was David Faustino, who would eventually break out in the role of Bud.

After our producer/writers had finally narrowed down a few choices for each part and Embassy Studio president Glenn Padnick signed off on them, we brought them all to one winner-take-all audition at FOX Studios in front of Barry Diller who, with his staff, had the final say. Even though FOX was billing itself as a different type of TV network, it wouldn't cede this traditional, all-important casting power to the studios or the writers. It's an old Hollywood conceit that there are moguls out there who have a sixth sense for discovering the right stars for the right parts and letting everything else sort itself out.

As happy as we were with our choices, we had two big fears going in to this session—the fact that we had initially lost Roseanne Barr and Sam Kinison might poison FOX against Katey Sagal and Ed O'Neill. Also, the actor you thought was perfect in your casting session will give a very different, less-than-whelming performance at the network and totally bomb.

Katey went first and eased our nerves with the same saucy, feisty audition that sold her on us in the first place. FOX loved her as well. Katey recalls the next phase of the network audition when she was paired with Ed in what's called a "chemistry read."

"I think she [the character Peggy] was really crazy about him. And I don't know if I just decided that or because I loved Ed so much. I loved being with Ed. He made me laugh and there was just that chemistry between us. I don't ever think it was a conscious thing as much as it just kind of *was*."

Ed, who felt the chemistry as well, was, much like his character, more blunt: "Katey likes men. She likes masculine men. And that's probably what she saw early on. That I was that kind of guy…this was a guy, a guy I liked."

Amanda Bearse said of her character, "Initially I based Marcy on my mother because when all else is falling down around her, my mother would just stand there smiling and that was sort of Marcy's experience in the pilot when she was introduced to the Bundys." She told me, however, that before this final audition, a studio executive offered her some "constructive criticism" on how to play the part that was quite different from her initial take, but "I trusted my performance that had gotten me this far, so I didn't change anything." Her trust, her instincts, and—in a way—her mom, were rewarded by getting the role.

Our picks for Bud and Kelly, Tina Caspary and Hunter Carson, were also easily approved at this audition. Now it was Ed O'Neill's big moment. Though this was an ensemble show, Al was clearly the red-hot center and, given the unique point of view of the series, he had a lot to carry. All eyes turned to the relatively inexperienced actor who began his audition with the same plaintive sigh that had so impressed Moye to begin with. "To me, the audition was all about timing," said O'Neill, remembering that moment, "and getting the jokes right. That's what I concentrate on. It's a lot different than real life. It's like fooling people into thinking something is real, and the more you can fool them the better it comes across." Ed followed through with a great audition, which had everyone "fooled,"…almost.

Glenn Padnick remembered the minute Ed's audition ended: "We turned to the FOX execs, including his (Diller's) trusted Garth Ancier and they all expressed their enthusiasm, except for that damned Diller. He said: 'He was good, mind you, but this part has to be cast perfectly.'" Padnick felt manipulated by Diller's comment: "That puts you in the position of either saying—we don't care about 'perfect.' Or, this man *is* 'perfect.' When it's put that way, you can't win. Either way, you're going to say something stupid."

"Then," as Andrew Susskind, Embassy's head of development remembers, "everyone was astonished when FOX's casting consultant, Susan Edelman, uttered three words to Diller that he had never heard: 'Barry, you're wrong.' She went on to add: "He's funny, he's sexy, he's relatable." To which Diller replied: "Okay, you heard what I had to say, now do what you want,'" and walked out of the room. Once Diller left, to everyone's relief, his people approved Ed O'Neill to play Al Bundy.

The minute Ancier returned to his office, however, Diller called to ask what happened after he walked out.

"We hired O'Neill," Garth told him.

Diller exploded: "Didn't you hear me say he's not the right guy?!"

Garth: "But you also said, 'do what you want.'"

Diller: "Yes, but I didn't mean it!"

What Diller did mean, as we rudely discovered the next morning, was—if we weren't willing to dump Ed O'Neill and cast someone else (never mind we had already seen every actor in town), FOX would reduce our thirteen episode, on-the-air, commitment to the traditional network model of one single episode, with an option for twelve more...*their* option. Simply put, either Padnick agreed to recast Ed O'Neill, or we would have to shoot one, make-or-break pilot to prove that Ed O'Neill was right for the part. If Diller still didn't like him, we'd be cancelled before we even aired. So much for the biggest advantage for everyone involved of taking the risk to work for a fledgling new network.

The fallout at Embassy Studios was strong. Andrew Susskind recalled that when FOX made the original offer to do *Married... With Children*, Gary Lieberthal, the top man at the studio, had said: "I don't know why we're doing a show with FOX. What the fuck is FOX and more importantly even if we did do a show for FOX it's not going to make any money?"

So it was no surprise that after this latest development, Lieberthal said: "What are we gonna do, what are we gonna do? Diller has spoken. We have to move on." Meaning, find another actor to play Al Bundy and keep the commitment on the books. Padnick, to his credit, had so much faith in Ed O'Neill and *Married... With Children*, he wouldn't be cowed by Barry Diller, or his own superiors who were invoking a bottom-line mentality to dump O'Neill, please FOX, and retain the much coveted and highly bankable thirteen episode on-the-air order. Leavitt and Moye were also dead set against recasting O'Neill.

It was no small feat for Glenn to stand up to Diller, whose uncertainty about casting Ed struck fear into the hearts of everyone who knew how bullish he was and to what lengths he would go to launch a successful fourth network. Mark Zakarin, who was next in line to head the marketing department at rival ABC at the time, remembers that Diller approached him about leaving ABC to become the head of marketing at FOX to help Barry get a competitive edge against the alphabet network, just as he had done in successfully poaching rising star, Garth Ancier from the programming department at NBC.

"Everyone knew Diller's reputation," Mark told me. "He was brilliant and brash and rude and crude. He was flossing his teeth while he was interviewing me. He looked at you from the corner of his eye, in a feral kind of way. Then he interrupted our interview to take a phone call from his mother, and he didn't ask me to leave the room. He just talked sweetly to his mother for a couple of minutes and then he returned to his edgy, feral, hyped-up self. He was a piece of work, that guy."

When Barry offered Mark the job, and he told Brandon Stoddard, his boss at ABC, that Diller was trying to steal him away, Brandon told him: "Diller is just trying to fuck with me and you too." Brandon, knowing Diller was serious, promptly promoted Mark to Head of Marketing at ABC to keep him from jumping ship. When Mark consequently turned Diller down because of his ABC promotion, Diller echoed Stoddard's response: "Brandon's fucking you…he's fucking you."

The one executive who refused to be *fucked* with by Diller, however, was Embassy Studio President Glenn Padnick, who stood his ground and refused to dump Ed O'Neill. Glenn, who was an integral part of the team that would one day put *Seinfeld* on the air, proudly maintains that standing behind O'Neill versus keeping the thirteen-episode commitment "was one of the few decisions I've made of any consequence. I said, we'll shoot episode one as though it were a pilot and see if Diller still wants to do it."

It was a ballsy move befitting a ballsy show. We plowed into production mode to make the best pilot we could, with the additional burden of having to convince a pissed-off Diller and a chastened FOX that Ed O'Neill was the best choice to play Al Bundy. Game on.

It's worth noting that even though TV pioneer Norman Lear had sold his interests in Embassy Studios a year before *Married... With Children* was created, most of the people involved in the show, including Glenn Padnick, Ron Leavitt, Michael Moye and myself had worked for Lear and were steeped in his trailblazing traditions.

CHAPTER 3

THE PILOT GAME: WE'RE NOT THE COSBYS AND THERE'S A GOOD CHANCE WE WON'T EVEN BE THE BUNDYS

RON AND MICHAEL HIRED LINDA Day to direct the *Married... With Children* pilot. Besides having directed over 350 TV episodes and being honored by the Directors Guild of America for paving the way for women in television, Linda was a very funny, extremely skilled director, as put-together and nurturing as Ron and Michael were scruffy and, to the uninitiated, intimidating.

On the first morning of a very tight, eight-day production schedule, after coffee, bagels, donuts and chit-chat, the network, studio, director, writers, and superfluous hangers-on assembled around a long table on a studio sound stage to hear a table reading. Aside from bits and pieces of dialogue in casting sessions, this is the first time anyone will have heard the entire script read aloud by the actors. Besides being charged with an air of expectation and electricity, this reading's practical and essential purpose is to give everyone involved a chance to flag any problem spots that may need rewriting before rehearsals begin in earnest.

Tensions were understandably high, as a great table read gives you momentum going into your pilot production while a bad one casts a noxious fog over your show that is hard to dispel. Plus, in our situation, we had the Ed O'Neill casting cloud hanging low over our heads.

As much at stake as there was, however, Ron Leavitt loved to kick off highly charged network events like this with squirm-inducing comedy bits. For example, Glenn Padnick told me that one time, Ron and his cocreators, Michael Moye and David Duclon, were meeting with the president of NBC to discuss casting the part of the father for the pilot they wrote for the show that would eventually become the hit series *Silver Spoons*. The network was sold on the child actor, Ricky Schroder, to play the son but they wouldn't commit to the series until they found the perfect father.

As it turned out, John Belushi had been found dead of an overdose that morning. With full knowledge of this going into the meeting, Ron engineered a bit of very dark humor where Dave Duclon, with a perfectly straight face, said to the NBC brass: "And the person we think would be perfect to play his father is John Belushi.' Word of Belushi's passing had only come out in the last hour, and there was a pall over the room. Then Ron pretended to whisper something into Dave's ear, to which Dave reacted with a *nod*, and then quickly said to the executives, 'Dan Ackroyd. Dan Ackroyd would be so perfect.'"

"It just broke up the room," Padnick remembers. "It just killed the room. And then it was smooth sailing. It was so wonderful to be on their side in that meeting."

In his introductory remarks at the *Married... With Children* pilot reading, Ron took dead aim at the ragtag, neophyte FOX network, mocking the fact that, at the time, FOX had UHF stations that required an antenna and were so far down the dial viewers couldn't find them, and even if they could, the reception was so weak they couldn't watch them. As a visual representation of this (precable and prestreaming) joke, for years, whenever the Bundy family gathered to watch a show on FOX TV as part of a scene in the series, Al would proclaim: "Assume FOX Network viewing positions" and the family members would each hold up coat hangers and crudely formed tinfoil antennae to get better reception.

Some felt Ron's subversive intros were a ploy to break the ice and get an otherwise stiff room of "suits" laughing. Network executives, despite their sworn duty as zookeepers for their shows, often long to be one of the animals. I personally think Ron just couldn't help spewing out his acerbic, social class–leveling humor, which rolled off his tongue like dialogue in *Married... With Children*.

That said, everyone enjoyed Ron's little roast and when the laughs subsided and the free snacks had been scarfed down, the script reading went well. There were a lot of big laughs, a few "crickets" (code for a line that gets so little response, you can hear the crickets chirping outside), and some minor story problems. Nothing we writers couldn't handle with a healthy (eight to ten hour) rewrite. Now, it was the dreaded time when traditionally the network gave us their notes about what they liked and didn't like about the script reading, but, as we know, this was in no way a traditional show or a traditional network.

Garth Ancier said that when he was first helping to put the network together, he knew he needed prestige, A-list writers like Jim Brooks (*The Mary Tyler Moore Show*), Steven Cannell (*The Rockford Files*) and Ed. Weinberger (*Cosby*). "But I also needed people who could do some stuff outside the box. So, I went to Leavitt and Moye's office and literally just got down on my knee and begged them to do a show for us. I knew the argument for Ron and Michael was freedom...you get to do something you want to do."

Ted Harbert remembers how ABC reacted to this *freedom* FOX was offering to snare viewers from them: "We understood FOX wanted to set themselves apart, which was smart. Specifically to *Married... With Children*, we were pretty shocked by some of the content, and I remember some jealousy because I knew that ABC Broadcast Standards and Practices Department [censors] would never allow language like that on our shows. I remember several 'how come they can do that and we can't' fights that would grow more heated during the *Roseanne* years. But the sales department always sided with Standards and Practices, saying that regardless of what FOX was peddling, 'We can't sell that stuff.'"

What FOX's "no notes" policy meant specifically to us was that, in practice, it could still give notes on our show but, ultimately, we didn't have to take them. That morning, after the pilot reading and an unusually perfunctory and polite network note session, we retreated to Ron and Michael's office—the writing room—to.share our own notes and begin a page-by-page rewrite of the problem spots we perceived from the table reading.

The concept that is often lost or misunderstood in the traditional battle between networks and writers, or any business that mixes art and commerce, is that the artist has the same interest in making the best final product as the "suits" do. "We didn't have a problem with notes," Michael Moye said, "we had a problem with notes that either made absolutely no sense or came from left field. If we understood them, we didn't have a problem with them."

To be fair, FOX's Garth Ancier was one of the few network executives I have ever worked with who was averse to giving a lot of notes. "There's this fallacy," Garth told me, "that some network executives have in their head that if you give enough notes to even just *okay* producers or writers that you'll get a great show. I've preached—if you have to give more than five notes to anyone, they shouldn't be running your show, because if you were that good of a writer, you would be making the shows instead of being an executive at the network."

After the reading, Ron and Michael and our motley writing crew, hunkered down in a writer's room—basically an executive office with couches and overstuffed chairs—for many hours, eating pizza, making obscene and, by today's standards, "actionable" jokes about each other, and rewriting the hell out of a script to make it as good as we possibly could…with or without network notes.

I had worked in many a writers' room but none compared to the atmosphere of Ron and Michael's. As *Playboy Magazine* noted in a feature article about the show: "Piles of paper litter the floor. A six-foot inflatable Frankenstein's monster looms in the shadows. A faded piñata dangles from the ceiling. Plastic weapons crowd a cabinet marked SANDINISTA PRO SHOP. The place looks more like a dorm room than an executive office, its collegiate atmospherics enhanced by the hussy-on-a-hog biker poster and especially by Leavitt's desk, a small, shabby lump buried in paper and topped with a dirty ashtray, a bottle of mouthwash and a king-size jar of antacid. It's in this murky squalor that the show's six staff writers and two executive producers cobble their antisitcom together."

Ron and Michael's playpen of an office also plays into another story that happened shortly after Coca-Cola coughed up $485 million to buy Embassy Studios back in 1985. The multinational soft drink giant sent a group of its top executives to Hollywood to check out their investment, or as Glenn Padnick, said: "To kick the tires on their new car." As Michael tells the story, when the executives got to Ron and Michael's office: "The looks on Coke's faces were priceless when they entered the room. They were definitely not prepared. Glenn then dutifully introduced us and after their eyes took it all in, they almost pleadingly looked back over at us when Ron proudly announced, '…And *we're* the best they've got!' I think they would've resold the outfit for half of what they paid for it, right then," Michael added. "Never saw 'em again either."

In spite of (or maybe because of) the toy-store trappings and cartoonish atmosphere, Ron and Michael ran an extremely focused, open, and diverse writing room, which extended to the staffing of the entire show. Predating network and guild diversity hiring requirements, *Married… With Children* employed a high percentage of women and people of color at all levels of production. Of the thirteen episodes in the first season, seven were written or cowritten by women, five were written or cowritten by African American writers, and twelve were directed by women.

The next afternoon, and every other day that week, the writers were called to the stage for a producer's run-through wherein the actors run through their lines and their camera blocking in a rehearsal hall, at about fifty percent of show-level intensity. The writer's job here is to look for ways to sharpen the jokes, make the story "track" (have continuity), and spot moments where the show is dragging and needs to be cut down. With each run-through and subsequent rewrite, the hope is that the script gets funnier, the actors more in character, and the show comes closer to being ready to perform in front of a live audience.

The run-throughs went well all week. After each scene, Ron and Michael gave the cast performance notes—a bit of a high-wire act because actors, like writers, can resent notes. Leavitt and Moye were brilliant at being open to what the actors had to say about the script, incorporating their suggestions into the dialogue and being hugely supportive in the process.

Ted McGinley, who would join the cast as a regular later in the run, said, "I would get down on myself blowing a line at run-through, and Ron and Michael would always make room for, *we* did it wrong. Could you help *us*? Ron was a guy who could rip your heart out with his wit in a matter of seconds, but when he was giving notes on stage he was all like, 'It's probably *us*, we didn't write this right, but could you change this?' Michael was the same way."

One of my favorite physical bits in the pilot was a result of the openness of Leavitt and Moye's inclusive rehearsal/run-through process. It comes after Peggy had been trying to manipulate Marcy into taking more control of Steve and we wanted to make sure the audience knew it had the desired effect of influencing her and, of course, disguise this intent by doing it as a joke. Earlier, the director featured Peggy rapidly kicking her leg up and down at a sharp angle while sitting on the couch as sort of a nervous tic. Now, to *show* rather than tell the audience that Peggy's attitude about Steve had, in fact, gotten through to the unwitting Marcy, we simply sat Marcy on the couch and had her exactly imitate Peggy's nervous leg kick, prompting a greater audience response than any verbal joke we could have written.

This sometimes arduous, often exhilarating run-through-rewrite-run-through-rewrite routine lasted all week. This writer-actor-director, give and take, was, to me, the best part of my job. It's like being at a hysterical live comedy show that you're watching and getting paid to work on at the same time.

After that day's run-through, we retreated to the writers' room where the rewriting and eating from Styrofoam boxes routine repeated itself...this time with huge, greasy meatball subs into which Ron, with the gleam in his eye of a master chef who just invented a new dish, inserted a row of potato chips between the roll and the meatballs, before he devoured the sandwich in a few gulps while hunched over the edge of a trash can that functioned like a grown man's bib, catching about as much of the meatball sub as Ron consumed. Ron was as meticulous with his writing as he was sloppy with his eating, though he enjoyed both more than anyone I know.

As a side note, one night after a run-through, years later, having tired of the usual take-out food we ordered nightly from nearby restaurants, Ron and Michael got an inspiration to send our production assistant, Carl Studebaker, to Dodger Stadium to get us Dodger Dogs and fries for dinner (no vegans, these two). When Carl got to the stadium gate, however, he encountered considerable resistance from the guard about simply buying the hot dogs to go; without having first bought a ticket to the game. "It took a lot of phone calls and a few bribes of *Married… With Children* swag to finally make it happen." Carl remembers. "Then I thought it would be a one and done deal, but once I showed everyone it was possible, they thought nothing of asking for it again."

Carl's can-do attitude did not go unnoticed or unrewarded. A few years later, when Ron and Michael were in the middle of negotiations for an unprecedented three-year $32 million deal, Carl told them that if he couldn't move up to another, better-paying job on the show, he was regrettably going to have to quit. Ron and Michael, according to Carl: "actually put it as a condition in their negotiations that I get promoted to a better job." Leavitt and Moye got their $32 million, Carl got his promotion, and Leavitt and Moye continued to forge a bond with their staff, crew, and actors on a show that was a big part of the reason that almost all of the people who worked on it have told me today that it was unquestionably the best job of their life…it certainly was mine.

CHAPTER 4

THE NETWORK RUN-THROUGH: WHEREIN FOX GETS PMS ABOUT PMS

A FEW DAYS LATER, IT was time for a rehearsal that was shared with the network. Nerves were understandably on edge for this network run-through because it was the first time FOX executives would see the show since the table reading, and the last time they would get an opportunity do anything about it before shooting the pilot. FOX was, so far, keeping its promise of not giving notes, which meant our pilot, to this point, had more edgy jokes and coarse language than would ever air on any other (non-FOX) network show. This unusual amount of creative freedom had the effect of immediately bonding us writers (and the crew and the actors) as a team, in a way that usually takes at least a full season, if at all, to accomplish. I was grateful but wary, thinking this hands-off policy was too good to be true, and damn if that wasn't prophetic.

As a matter of practice, good censors rarely give notes on specific jokes or lines of dialogue until they hear them *on their feet*, literally and figuratively, at the network run-through. The theory being that a live, nuanced, performance can give a borderline inappropriate joke a totally different tone and *feel* than it has on the page. At this particular run-through, besides evaluating the quality of the show, we were paying close attention to any potentially "censorable" lines. Trade secret: writers and crew are cautioned not to *overlaugh* any particularly off-color joke at the run-through, to avoid flagging it for the censors.

The network run-through takes place on the stage and in the sets where it will soon be shot, so we can also judge the set dressing and the blocking. The half dozen or so executives from FOX and a similar number from our studio, plus the writing staff and the crew function as a make-shift audience, whose laughter (or silence) is a barometer for whether or not the script is working. Even though this performance still isn't at peak performance level for the actors, the expectations are much higher than the initial table reading, particularly since, in this case, the pilot was going to be shot the next day and there was, consequently, much less time to fix any problem spots that might come up. The tension was palpable.

In one early exchange, Peg tells Al how proud she is of the kids. He replies:

AL: I'm sorry, honey, I didn't hear you. I was just thinkin' of killing myself.

Big laugh and the censors have absolutely no problem with this suicide joke, which would never fly on any other show back then (and certainly not now) but was saved by Ed's perfectly nonchalant, self-deprecating, facetious delivery, not to mention Peggy's deadpan response.

PEGGY: Not tonight, honey, we have company coming over.

This line, besides being funny, frees the audience to laugh because if Peggy doesn't take Al's threat seriously, neither should we. In the future, this "I've heard it all before," tone would give license to a world of otherwise impossible jokes, but soon, it would be unclear if the Bundys would even have a future.

Toward the end of act two, Al and Steve are alone on the couch as Steve drones on about how perfect newlywed Marcy is. Al, of course, has a different point of view of marriage from his wide-eyed neighbor as he cautions Steve to not say anything critical of his wife,

AL: ...or else they'll kill you. And they're allowed to, see it's that whole period, PMS thing, I don't know, I'm not a doctor, but I think that PMS stands for "Pummel Men's Scrotums."

This gets a big laugh and we move on to a parallel scene in the kitchen where Marcy drones on about how perfect newlywed Steve is. Then Peggy gets Marcy to admit that Steve has started going to bed later and getting up earlier than she does. Peggy stirs the pot (not literally—she doesn't even own one), cautioning Marcy that Steve having a good time by himself is the beginning of the end of their marriage. Fortunately, Peggy, has a thoughtful tip for her new friend:

PEGGY: Do you have PMS?

MARCY: No.

PEGGY: Get it.

Weaponizing PMS isn't your traditional sitcom "neighborly" advice, but because Peggy delivers it in a matter-of-fact fashion, with the perfect amount of the sly, internal wink of her character, it also gets solid laughs and FOX's censors also seem fine with Peggy's PMS joke.

The rest of the run-through went great. The handful of FOX executives present thought it was very funny. Their censors didn't give us any more notes. Katey and Ed were hysterical. Amanda and David were excellent. Tina Caspary and Hunter Carson, though not stellar, were not enough of a concern to think about replacing...yet.

"Baron Von Diller," unfortunately, wasn't there to witness Ed's fine performance and perhaps change his mind about him, but it wasn't unusual for a top network executive to save his or her single, regal appearance for the pilot taping itself. Still, we could foresee Diller getting a very good report on O'Neill from his minions. What we did not foresee, however, was that FOX, on Diller's behalf, was about to go back on their promise *not* to censor the show. It now dropped a bomb on us that could have easily killed the series when it maintained that, even though Peggy had her own *acceptable* PMS joke, Al's line, "PMS stands for Pummel Men's Scrotums" was over FOX's line and insisted we cut it.

Garth Ancier, our closest ally in the FOX camp, immediately set a meeting to try to make peace, but Ron Leavitt didn't mince his words about FOX mincing *their* words: "You told us to be free. Now you tell us not to be free. Which is it?" Ancier was apologetic but made it clear he did not come to negotiate a settlement. Diller hated the joke, so either we cut it or change it, or they would shut down the show. Michael and Ron, though feeling betrayed and mightily pissed off, eventually figured that, on balance, we still had a very edgy show with plenty of their original, satirical vision intact, so we made the concession and cut the line.

The only thing left for us to do now was, no less than the single hardest thing we had to do from the start—shoot the pilot in front of a live audience. On top of everything else that had to fall in place on that one night, we had to make sure a dubious Barry Diller thought Ed O'Neill was the living embodiment of Al Bundy, or *Married... With Children* would never be seen on the FOX Network…even in the few cities where the ragtag network had good reception.

POSTSCRIPT—PUMMEL THIS, FOX!

One unexpected consequence of the PMS incident was that, whatever we lost in laughs by having the line, "Pummel Men's Scrotums" cut from our script, we gained in the bonding that the censorship fostered on our stage. I say this because, a little while later, our stage crew, in the guise of a birthday surprise for someone on stage, had a large, pink, papier-mâché piñata built in the shape of a man's scrotum (complete with black, stringy pubic hairs), and hung it from the lighting grid. Then, providing a bat and a blindfold, they allowed the crew, the cast and whoever else was around, to physically do to the piñata what we were forbidden to so much as *say* in our script—pummel men's scrotums.

Without getting too philosophical, this creative, well-coordinated, labor-intensive stunt was so much in keeping with *Married... With Children*'s bold sense of humor and defiant tone that it signaled to me that the crew already identified so strongly with Al and the sensibility of the show that they felt when we lost the joke, *they* did too. Or, they may just have been craving the candy that was stuffed inside the piñata. Either way, a good time was had by all, and the bonding process so essential to a demanding group mission like this was off to an early start.

The crew, emboldened by the community spirit of the workplace, which flowed from Michael and Ron at the top, continued to express their sense of humor and comradeship through their jobs. For example, a few years later, in the episode, "All Night Security Dude," Al gets hired by his old high school as a night security watchman and has a standoff with his arch high school football rival, "Spare Tire Dixon," played by All-Pro defensive end Bubba Smith, who is trying to steal Al's hard-earned city championship football trophy from the trophy case. As Al and "Spare Tire" try to prove who deserves the trophy most on the basis of who had the *worst* life after that championship game, they each pull out their wallets and show each other pictures of their dreaded mothers-in-law. Unbeknownst to either actor, Adrian Cranny and Mike Semon of our prop department inserted photos they obtained of plus-sized women in sexy underwear into the actors' wallet compartments. When the actors pulled out their pictures to show each other, they both saw the raunchy photos for the first time and totally broke character and couldn't stop laughing. After everyone on the set also shared in the laugh, the scene was shot for real and everyone felt more connected than they ever were.

Though practical jokes like this were occasionally played to break tension and create unity on the set, they were permitted only because Ron and Michael knew how prepared, disciplined, and dedicated everyone was to their jobs, and because when *laughter* is your stock and trade, why should it simply be the domain of your actors and your script?

CHAPTER 5

SHOOTING THE PILOT: BARRY, YOU'RE STILL WRONG

A SITCOM LIKE *MARRIED... WITH Children* is shot with multiple cameras (four, to be exact) on a stage in front of a live audience, like a play. This audience is assembled by giving free tickets to tourists and local shoppers at malls and other public places. The idea is to gather a collection of so-called "average viewers" to get a true read on whether your show works with the people for whom it's intended—random shoppers at the mall. Tonight, our "average" audience had been waiting outside in the cold for over an hour before finally being escorted in to sit on bleacher seats and watch a show, the likes of which they'd never seen, starring a cast they'd most likely never heard of, on which millions of dollars, hundreds of jobs and careers—in many ways, an entire TV network—were riding on.

Though multicamera shows, with few exceptions, are out of style today, this live audience form was thought, for many years, to benefit from the spontaneous give-and-take that springs forth from actors performing in a live arena. The process also allows you to objectively gauge whether your jokes are working. It's a simple equation applied to a complex problem—either your audience is laughing or it's not. Additionally, since the writers are right there on the stage while the show is being taped, if any given line doesn't work, there is an opportunity to rewrite it on the fly and shoot it again while the audience is still assembled. It's a real-time, trial-and-error process that you can't get in a single-camera, nonaudience show.

Critics, however, believe the trend in favor of single-camera comedies like *Schitt's Creek* and *Abbott Elementary* that are shot and edited like little movies instead of stage plays arose because many multicamera comedies weren't delivering on their promise to be funny. Flat reactions from the live audience were made even more evident when the producers added phony, canned laugh tracks and corny musical stings after the fact, in post-production, making the home audience feel manipulated or talked down to. On *Married... With Children*, the opposite was true—we never added laugh tracks. In fact, our audiences were so raucous we often had to let their laughter and hooting die down before continuing with the sequence or the show would run too long to be broadcast.

After our pilot audience had been "loaded in," a term that always makes me laugh for its association with cattle and cargo, the curtain went up on the opening scene. We held our collective breath and braced for the moment we'd been preparing for over these many months, which all came down to these next few hours, the judgement of a few hundred freeloading mall rats, and, of course, Barry Diller, who brought a tension of his own to the evening.

Prior to going out in front of the audience that night, Ed flashed on the fact that "I knew Diller didn't want me. I knew it was a high-wire act going in. But I didn't give a damn. I could care less." What Ed did give a damn about was being funny in front of this make-or-break audience because, as he put it, "in drama you don't know if it's working, because there's no laughs, but in comedy, you find out pretty fucking quick."

The opening scene has Peg seated at the table. Kelly sits on the couch. Al is offstage. The potted plant behind the couch "moves" towards Kelly. Bud jumps out from behind the plant where he was hiding, yanks on his sister's hair, and scares her half to death by pulling her head back while sliding a toy knife scary looking enough to get you thrown off an airplane across her defenseless neck. Peggy notices the skirmish but, unlike a typical sitcom mom, she chooses to snidely comment on his behavior rather than actually try to pull Bud off of his frightened sister like a *real* parent would.

> **PEGGY:** Bud, stop sneaking up behind your sister, pulling her hair, pretending to kill her. Do you remember the effect it had on Grandma? Nobody likes it. Nobody thinks it's funny, so cut it out, okay?

Bud dutifully removes the knife from Kelly's jugular vein. Then the Bundy siblings exchange rote I-hate-yous and go off to school. We get some scattered laughs, but it's a regrettably slow start. Then, Al enters, trying to staunch the flow of blood caused when he spiked his hand on a cactus plant that Peggy put where the alarm clock used to be. The audience is worrisomely tentative at this point—not sure if they should laugh or squirm.

This is the risk we took in going against the audience's expectations of a traditional sitcom. At this point, our "typical viewers," were probably wondering what happened to the amiable type of dad they were used to enjoying, like *Cosby*'s Cliff Huxtable or *Growing Pains*' Jason Seaver.

Katey Sagal said that she wasn't entirely taken off guard by the audience's confused, initial reaction to the material that opening night: "It was so different. I didn't have high expectations. If they hadn't responded or didn't laugh, I would not have been surprised. I thought this was way too out there for people who have been seeing family television a certain way. I'm kind of rebellious myself so I sort of liked all that. So, I said, let's give it to them and see what happens."

What did happen, fortunately, was that gradually, insult by insult, joke by joke, each layer of the character onion was peeled back until we started winning the audience over. Al's rejoinder to Peggy, late in the first scene, about how his back hair: "...keeps you offa' me at night," broke the dam and scored big laughs.

The brazenness of the lines combined with how Al and Peggy are still magnetically drawn to each other projects a sense that the characters, in spite of the hostile jokes, are just fine with each other. This gives the audience permission to laugh freely, which they did. Their positive energy, in turn, fueled Ed and Katey's performance, revving up the audience even more, which is the beauty and the essence of the multicamera form. Then, when you least expected it, after a few more high-and-inside fastballs, Peggy threw a major changeup:

PEGGY: Al, let's not start. We were having such a nice morning.

AL: Yeah, I'm sorry, you're right.

This gets a big laugh because it proves, as one critic from the *Los Angeles Times* noted, that "Peg and Al Bundy bandy insults and wish out loud the other would die or run away with the circus, but, as the audience knows, they are destined to torture each other as husband and wife forever." And, if the audience enjoyed what the Bundys were calling a "nice" morning, they'd certainly look forward to seeing what a "nasty" one looks like.

Speaking of nasty, the next scene is at the shoe store, where we first discover how Al is cursed to work as a lowly shoe salesman and also how he copes. Al waits on a woman customer, his trusty foot-measuring device at his side, and we witness the first wave of what will eventually be a tsunami of rough, often brutal exchanges between Al and female shoppers.

WOMAN: (rudely) I don't care what your little ruler says, I've been a seven since I graduated from high school!

AL: Well, these are sevens. The box says nine because well, uh…look, lady, you're a nine! I can accept it, why can't you?

WOMAN: You're very fresh!

Al: No, ma'am, that's impossible. 'Cause for the last hour, I've been trying to squeeze your foot into a shoe,

when really I should've been easing them into the box.
So, I'm anything but fresh.

The audience howls. Later, Ed, and a variety of critics, would theorize about why he felt his character could get away with these harsh insults without the audience turning on him. "If I made fun of a woman in the shoe store," Ed said, "it could never be my idea…I couldn't just *start* insulting them. It had to be out of desperation. A defensive, *get-off-me* kind of thing, where they would be horrendous customers. If it wasn't that, it didn't work." Ed said he was nonetheless uncomfortable making fun of women's appearances. "I would always say to the women in the rehearsal, 'This is very difficult for me to do, and I don't enjoy it, but, it is kind of funny.' They were like, 'It's fine. It's how I got the job.' They understood it, but, it certainly wasn't fun to do it."

"*Married… With Children* was meant to shock," Christina Applegate would later tell *E! True Hollywood Story* in a piece about the show after she had been added to the cast. "And I'm not offended by it whatsoever. I mean, that's like saying you'd be offended by *All in the Family*." The irony is that Archie Bunker's show was considered progressive and biting, while *Married* was considered lowbrow and decadent, even though Archie was, in fact, every bit, if not more, as politically incorrect as Al:

ARCHIE: Women was created for two things: makin' meals and babies. Why do you think the cave women was created with short legs and fat butts? So they couldn't run fast. So the men could catch 'em and force 'em to make the meals and the babies.

The point is, you're supposed to laugh with Archie and Al, not emulate them. As Ed observed: "The show is so deliberately cartoonish. The last thing I think Al should be is a role model. Were Laurel and Hardy role models? Is Elmer Fudd a role model?" If there is such a thing as poetic justice, Diana Bellamy, who played the customer from the pilot, came back ten years later in the final season to lead a group of similarly insulted-by-Al-women, tied him to a chair, and put him on trial for "Crimes Against Obesity." This led to more insults, but at least she got her shots in, and her character had come full circle.

The debate over the show's appropriateness would play out in many forms over the years, but at this point in the pilot performance, we had managed to jolt tonight's audience out of their traditional expectations, make them forget they were missing Friday night at the mall, and the rest of the pilot was electric. The now "all in" audience especially loved the finale, where Al and Peggy succeed in inciting a fight between Steve and Marcy that ultimately shoots them out the door, leaving Al and Peggy so unexpectedly aroused that they go upstairs and have sex. As CNN would point out almost thirty-five years later in *The History of the Sitcom*: "This idea of a darker family presentation spoke to people who were bored with what the main family sitcoms were offering at the time." *Married* may have been a lot of things, but it was clearly not your "main family sitcom."

As the actors took their curtain call to thunderous applause, I finally allowed myself to feel that we had a shot at becoming a series, but none of us had any inkling how much impact it would ultimately have. Our goal was simply to push the boundaries of traditional family comedy to the limit, crash the traditional network's party, and have a blast doing it…we did and we were.

We did have some concerns, however, about the actors playing the Bundy kids early in the rehearsal phase and once we edited together the pilot, it became obvious that the brute comic force of Ed and Katey's performance made the kids come off as way too vulnerable. This undermined the comedy in the scenes they were in and clearly signaled a problem for the future—you wouldn't laugh at the edginess of Al and Peggy if you were too busy feeling sorry for Bud and Kelly. So, we set out to quickly recast the kids, reshoot their scenes, and edit them into the version of the pilot that we would ultimately deliver to FOX.

Enter Christina Applegate and David Faustino. David had auditioned for the part earlier but, for whatever reason, didn't make the cut. This time, however, "When Faustino came in with that baby face but pretty much the eyes of evil," Michael Moye remembers, "we knew that he would work." Michael was also impressed that David, unlike the other young actors who read for the part, didn't "laugh at his own jokes after he delivered them," a rare quality in a kid actor.

Christina was originally considered for the part as well, but she initially thought the script was "disgusting" and didn't even audition. Furthermore, "When they came back to me," Applegate said, "I was like 'Nooooo!' And they sent me the tape of the pilot and my mom and I did not want to like it, and we were stifling laughter. So I thought I'll go in, but I'd never done comedy before."

Turns out she didn't have to, because when she came in to audition, Moye recalls, "…her hair was so blonde it was almost white. She had a black studded leather jacket on, and I said, 'Hell, if this kid can speak English she's the front runner.' She was so different from the usual sitcom fare and trying to turn it on its head." More importantly, Moye added, she was someone who you could believe had all those edgy "attributes but nevertheless you'd never expect to find her hooked on meth or carrying some stoner's baby. This was not an easy role to cast. Not even in Hollywood."

In spite of Christina's lack of experience and self-doubt about her comedy skills, she was naturally very funny and earned the opportunity to audition for the network. So, with David, Christina, and several other promising young actors in tow, we went back to FOX for another casting session, this time to approve the new, brattier, Bundyesque Bud and Kelly.

David Faustino vividly remembers that when they got to the final audition at the network and he was paired with Christina, it clicked right away. "I could tell from the reactions in the room, particularly Ron and Michael, that I was in top contention for the job." David also remembered, right after the audition, going down in the elevator with his mom and one of the other boys who had auditioned who was accompanied by his mother as well. "The kid had flown in from New York, and he asked his mom, 'Whether or not I get the part, can we still toast with champagne tonight?'" This was a sure sign to David that this kid didn't feel like he was going to get the part and needed to drown his underage sorrow in some bubbly. David's instincts, like his acting choices, were right on the money, and he and Christina both got the parts.

We went to reshoot the scenes, which were fortunately, relatively isolated from the rest of the show. Though we were completely taken with Christina's comedic chops during these reshoots, Christina was very insecure about it herself and remembers, "I know that my mom said to Ed O'Neill on day one, 'Look, Christina's not very good at comedy, will you help her?' I guess eventually I figured it out."

Having reshot the kids' scenes, we promptly cut them into the pilot and then delivered the final product to FOX for what we hoped would be its ultimate approval of the series. FOX responded positively to David and Christina, and Barry Diller finally agreed that Ed O'Neill was the right choice to play Al.

Everything looked good, until, as so predictably happens before the final resolution in a sitcom plot, there was one more obstacle to overcome before there could be a happy ending. FOX, which had originally promised not to judge the show by traditional standards, decided to resort to the ultimate traditional standard—audience testing—and wouldn't officially approve the show until Leavitt and Moye came in to listen to the test results and agreed to make changes accordingly. This felt, to Ron and Michael, like they were reliving the PMS situation all over again.

Before a traditional network puts a show on the air, it "tests" it by screening it to a small sample audience hooked up to electronic devices to record real-time reactions to the show. Participants then engage in a panel discussion led by a research "expert," sharing opinions about whether they would watch the show. Based on their reactions, the "experts" create graphs and formulas as predictors of the show's success or failure in the marketplace.

TV executives like testing because they are risk-averse, and it appears to quantify something that is otherwise ineffable. Writers hate it for the same reason, and also because it is often a terrible predictor of success, especially with shows that aren't right down the middle of an audience's expectations. *Seinfeld* is among the many shows that tested poorly yet became big hits. The test audience felt it wasn't funny, they hated Jerry, and said he needed a better backup ensemble.

Leavitt and Moye were also furious because FOX had once again gone back on a promise. I recall Ron saying: "If we wanted to have our show tested, we would have taken it to a *real* network." They didn't want to go in to hear the results but Garth Ancier, who had counseled them through the PMS crisis, told them that, as sympathetic as he was to their point of view, they had no choice—if they wanted the show to get on the air, they had to take the meeting…so they did.

Moye recalls the event: "I remember walking in…this was like a Warner Brothers' cartoon meeting room to me. This had one of these long tables you'd only see on TV. This went on forever and I'm thinking, there's not enough people who work here to even fill up this table. We each sat down, and we each had a little manila folder in front of us. At the end of the table there was an easel, then *Professor Somebody* came in, and we went through a bunch of charts and graphs. And we learned that people born in August liked this. And people who wore blue shirts liked this. People who drove Dodges liked this. And when the professor reached a summation, because that's about all I heard, he said we needed to: '…make Al and Peggy clearly more love each other and the kids clearly love their parents and the family more supportive and more loving.'" In other words, everything we were dedicated to satirizing.

Then Ron Leavitt shot back with a line that is still quoted in TV writer circles and would have gone viral had there been social media at the time: "You, sir, are why television sucks." The meeting abruptly ended and, "If they did more testing," according to Moye, "they wisely didn't say anything more to us." Diller gave the green light and ordered the full thirteen episodes of *Married... With Children*.

Barry may have argued strongly against Ed O'Neill while we were casting the pilot, but "Years later," Ed remembers, "'I ran into Diller and he came up to me, and he said, 'You know, I made a mistake about you.' And I said, 'Well, we all make 'em.'"

POSTSCRIPT—*MARRIED* MEETS THE PRESS

FOX, prior to the official launch of their network, had been running the Joan Rivers talk show, *The Late Show*, as a trial balloon for several months before broadcasting its scripted shows and kicking off the network in earnest. Now armed with several scripted shows, including ours, FOX gathered all of its TV station affiliates from around the country and all of the entertainment press it could round up to make a much ballyhooed formal presentation of its premier lineup, even though the programming did not yet fill a full week's schedule. FOX, with comparatively limited resources and no broadcast history, was counting on the affiliate and press screenings to create buzz for its debut. What they didn't count on was that *Married... With Children* would provide the defining moment of the press conference itself.

Rob Kenneally, who was working for FOX Studios' television production arm at the time, recalled the press conference in Los Angeles. "They had announced and walked up on stage everybody who was anybody in the writer/producer series world. It was, `We are all embracing this network, we who could work anywhere have decided to come to FOX to do our next new show.' So, Cannell went up, Spelling went up, Gary David Goldberg had come up, Jim Brooks had come up. And then there were these two guys who were relatively unknown, Michael Moye and Ron Leavitt. They were sort of the next rung or two down from the guys that were previously on stage. Unlike everyone else who had done an almost spiritual presentation of how important a fourth network was, Michael and Ron get up to the podium."

"We told them that we really didn't have anything prepared," Michael said "and we're not gonna blow smoke up your ass like these other guys. But we can promise you this, we're not trying to teach anyone a lesson through this show, or set anyone's moral compass, or tell you how to vote, or even tell you which brand of toilet paper to buy." Then, Michael asks the crowd, "How many out there have children?' A bunch of people raised their hands. Then Ron says, 'And how many of you just can't wait to get home to these little shits? That's what our show is about.'"

The room exploded with laughter and then Ed. Weinberger, cocreator of *The Cosby Show* and the writer who created *Mr. President* (starring George C. Scott) for this new FOX lineup, took the mic from Ron and got a huge laugh when he said: "I want to work on *that* show." Weinberger was either unaware of or unconcerned at the time with the delightful irony that the original title of *Married... With Children* was, *We're Not the Cosbys*.

CHAPTER 6

SEASON 1: HURRAY FOR F-O-X-Y-W-O-O-D

On Sunday, April 5, 1987, at 7:00 PM eastern time, the FOX Broadcasting Company launched its first prime-time series lineup with the pilot episode of *Married… With Children*, the show it almost cancelled before it was even shot. To celebrate the occasion, FOX hosted a glitzy, star-studded premiere party on a high-rise rooftop, in full view of the world-famous Hollywood Sign. Writers, cynical as we are, love to attend these lavish, VIP events for the opportunity to feel like we are part of the glamorous, public side of show business—instead of the dark, largely anonymous, cloistered side where we usually reside…and for the free food and drink.

We were told by our FOX hostesses as we arrived, that at exactly 7 PM, something magical would "light up the sky" to herald the launch. At that moment, as we would soon discover, FOX had arranged with the City of Los Angeles (over the strenuous objection of local homeowners) to transform the brightly lit letters of the iconic Hollywood Sign from, H-O-L-L-Y-W-O-O-D to F-O-X. This *not-so-special* effect did little to wow the crowd or distract our focus from the buffet table and open bar, but it no doubt inspired others who would later transform the letters of the Hollywood Sign to spell H-O-L-L-Y-B-O-O-B and H-O-L-L-Y-W-E-E-D to publicize their respective causes, though, unlike F-O-X, didn't bother to get permits for their stunts and were arrested for their efforts.

According to Brian Lowry, who was covering FOX for the *Hollywood Reporter* at the time, changing the sign to F-O-X was not all the network did to impress the media at the event: "The thing I always remember, it seemed like the PR department was full of twenty-year-old runway models. Everyone there looked really young and gorgeous." FOX may have been a disruptive network in many ways, but they stuck to some time-honored Hollywood traditions in others.

The initial broadcast of *Married... With Children* that night was directly followed by the pilot of *The Tracey Ullman Show*, then two more screenings of the same *Married... With Children* episode, sandwiched between two more repeats of the same *Tracey Ullman Show* episode. This highly unorthodox, repetitive "rollout," according to FOX network CEO Jamie Kellner, would allow potential TV viewers to "sample FOX programming without having to miss *60 Minutes* or *Murder, She Wrote*." FOX's thoughtfulness, however, was not reciprocated in kind, as *Murder, She Wrote* and *60 Minutes* buried *Married... With Children* and *The Tracey Ullman Show*'s debut in the Nielson rankings.

Ed O'Neill likened *Married*'s premier for the FOX network to the shock troops that first hit the beach in Normandy in WWII: "They knew they weren't going to survive. They were gonna bring the big guns up afterwards. This was cannon fodder. That's what I think they thought of *Married... With Children*, because they already had the backup shows with George C. Scott and Patty Duke and Tracey Ullman that Diller was counting on. We were just going to go in. Make a shock. Get mowed the fuck down. Then our bodies would be scattered on the beach and they'd bring in the big guns. They could never have imagined that we would outperform all of them and neither could I."

To make things worse, critics' reviews, with some notable exceptions, were almost as cool as the ratings. Tom Shales of the *Washington Post* called us out for being vulgar and crass: "It's like '*Who's Afraid of Virginia Woolf?*' in a tiny, teeny, infinitesimal way. Besides, *that* had a point." Though TV writers often decorate their office walls with negative reviews of new shows that eventually become huge hits, like *Seinfeld* and *How I Met Your Mother*, I admit to sitting in our heady, junk food–filled cocoon wondering how far a network sitcom, even one trying to distinguish itself on an unknown network, can really go? When does taking shots at sacred cows cross the line from funny to cruel? Was our guiding principle that Al and Peggy's derisive jokes were giving voice to what the person on the street is really thinking, but afraid to say out loud, really true, or was it simply the writer monkey in us flinging shit at the gawking zoo patrons?

After all, at the time, TV viewers were flocking to the family-friendly *Cosby Show, Growing Pains*, and *Family Ties*. Just two years prior, Tipper Gore's watchdog group, Parents Music Resource Center, held congressional hearings that forced the music industry to put stickers on rock albums, warning parents of "Explicit Content." Into this landscape blew *Married... With Children*, blithely joking about lust, greed, sloth, masturbation, and nudie bars.

Garth Ancier tried to reassure us that time was our ally: "Comedies always take longer to take hold with the audience because they take knowledge of the characters to see what is funny." The other thing we felt *time* would provide was the recognition and comfort that, as shocking as our tone was, we stayed scrupulously faithful to the traditional structure and visual style of the very sitcom form we were mocking. *Married* was basically saying, "We know the family comedy genre is a bunch of crap and you know it too, so let's have some fun with it together." "*Married... With Children*," as TV critic Jackson Upperco put it, "was not disrupting the format, it was disrupting the content. It was playing in the same sandbox as other sitcoms. It was abiding by the same rules."

For example, in the pilot, when Steve and Marcy first meet the Bundys, they innocently ask where their kids are? Al shrugs.

AL: I don't know.

And the audience howls with laughter at a throwaway comment that doesn't even resemble a traditional punch line. Why? Because, after years of watching family comedies, viewers already know what the pesky neighbors don't—that however dismissive Al is of his kids, he is still firmly rooted in a sitcom world where parents have to love their offspring, no matter what atrocities against each other or mankind they commit.

Then again, in the climax of the pilot, where in a typical Golden Moment, a sitcom couple earnestly resolves their fight with a pledge to do better, a plea for forgiveness, or an expensive necklace, Al and Peggy resolve theirs by fomenting a fight between Steve and Marcy, reinforcing a bond that leads to an

RICHARD GURMAN

unusual round of sex for the Bundys. This practice of building
on and honoring a popular genre, while simultaneously beating
the hell out of it had been very successfully popularized in film—
Blazing Saddles, *Airplane*, and *Fright Night*—but was still unfa-
miliar territory in the mid-1980s television landscape.

To visually reinforce the concept that *Married* was built on
the foundation of traditional sitcoms, according to Gerry Cohen,
who directed over half of our episodes: "We tended to give the
audience one porthole, one window into the lives of these folks
and that was in the imaginary fourth wall over the TV. You felt
comfortable as an audience because your orientation was your
regular point of view and we rarely turned it on its ear." Thus,
without the audience consciously realizing it, we employed a traditional visual style they could comfortably be grounded in while
our storytelling went through the roof.

The second episode of Season 1 picks up where the pilot left
off—chipping away at sitcom tropes like "married couples are
still hot for each other" and also fueling the rivalry between Al
and Marcy. The story centers on Marcy convincing a frustrated
Peggy that Al's waning interest in sex would be rejuvenated by
feeding him the recipes in the self-help cookbook *Thinnergy*.

AL: Your wife gave my wife a book. Now my life is hell.

STEVE: Ah…*Thinnergy*.

AL: Yeah, that's the one. Does Marcy hate me
that much?

STEVE: Well yes, Al, she does.

Of course, this strategy doesn't work and drives the Bundys even farther apart. Then, when all seems lost, we apply the *Married* satirical treatment to what Michael Moye calls the traditional sitcom "make-up moment": *Yes, I've been acting like an idiot, but (LOOKS AT WATCH) we've got thirty-three seconds but I love you and I love the kids and lets all hug.* Instead, you get:

> **AL:** Oh honey, just 'cause I don't go to bed with you doesn't mean I don't love ya. I mean, let's face it, even if you were beautiful, like that girl on TV, I'd still ignore ya, 'cause you're my wife. (PEGGY LOOKS AT HIM) Don't stiffen on me, Peg. Let me tell you what I mean: you remember that baseball glove my dad gave me when I was a little kid? (PEGGY NODS) I love that glove. Yeah, it's old and the web's loose, but it's special to me. That's how I feel about you, Peg. I love you. I think you're great. Just the way you are. (THEY KISS.) So's my glove. (SHE KISSES HIM AGAIN).

As offensive and atypical as it sounds for a husband to compare his wife to a worn-out piece of leather, Al's speech, coming exactly where it would in a typical sitcom resolution and affirmed as a positive by how Peggy's kisses, evince a collective "aww" from our audience who are now in on the joke. They know that, as unpolished and crude as Al is, he would no sooner get rid of Peg (or his glove) as Cliff Huxtable would of Clair or Stephen Keaton would of Elyse.

Happily, the more shows we aired, the more viewers came to trust and recognize the traditional moments but twisted manner in which the Bundys express their bond, and, correspondingly, the bigger laughs we got. And, also according to plan, as over-the-top as Al is, Peggy could always go toe to toe with him. For example, later Peggy gives her own version of Al's baseball glove analogy to Marcy.

> **PEGGY:** Have you ever had a pair of old shoes? They're boring and ugly and stink to high heaven. But they're yours, you know? They're worn down and broken in and...and when you put 'em on it feels like there's nothing there, ha ha ha. That's my Al.

As out of the box as the first season was, it would be decidedly tamer than the following years of the series. Peggy had not completely turned her back on feeding her family, as when we hear the oven timer go off, and Al is hopeful.

> **AL:** You cooked?

> **PEGGY:** Nah, it's just a reminder to order dinner.

Al is still drawn to having sex with Peg, albeit infrequently, as we discover when Steve says:

> **STEVE:** Peggy, Al, I hope we aren't interrupting anything.

> **AL:** Naw, just a little sex with the wife. But what the hell, there's always next month.

In this first season, before Bud and Kelly grew into the brash, selfishly annoying kid roles they would become known for and which distinguished them from traditional sitcom kids (even bratty ones), we focused primarily on the marital squabbles between Al and Peggy and the divide-and-conquer relationship they had with their next-door nemeses, Steve and Marcy. For example, in "Whose Room is it Anyway," when the Bundys discover the Rhoadeses are planning to add on to their house, Al and Peggy take their counterparts aside and respectively try to con them into building a room for their own selfish purposes. After Al tries to convince Steve to make it a pool room that the two of them could use, Steve says,

> **STEVE:** I don't know. I think we should get a room we both like.

> **AL:** Well, she's got one. She's got the kitchen!

Meanwhile, when Peggy urges Marcy to build an exercise room that the two of them could use, Marcy replies,

> **MARCY:** Okay. I don't know, Peggy. Steve and I wanted a room we could both use.

> **PEGGY:** Oh, Steve has his own room. He has the kitchen!

In this first season, as we continued to play upon the overall Bundy/Rhoades dynamic in various episodes, we discovered that the audience was most responsive to the more heated, more focused Al and Marcy rivalry, inspiring many full-blown stories as well as a steady dose of gratuitous shots at each other, as when Al opens the front door and finds Marcy there:

> **AL:** Marcy, why are you here?

> **MARCY:** I wanted to talk to Peggy privately.

AL: No, no, why here, on earth?

"I loved Marcy and embraced whatever quirkiness the writers came up with," Amanda Bearse admitted, in spite of the eventual misgivings she would eventually express about some of the content of the show. "As with anything, it's about having fun. If you are, the audience will be too. It was often fun playing opposite Al."

No one took the idea of the show lasting very long, no less becoming one of the biggest hits on TV, seriously. "I really thought, this is way too far out for network television," Katey Sagal recalled. "Plus it was on FOX which was a little puny network that you didn't even get in most households. At that point, I was just pleased to be employed, because I had worked as a freelance musician for so much of my twenties, but I didn't think long-term at all."

Katey wasn't the only one in Hollywood making fun of FOX's future and its technical ability to reach most viewers. ABC's top dog Ted Harbert reflected our competition's cynicism about the viability of FOX when he was honored for his service as president of the prestigious Hollywood Radio and Television Society with an Ollie Award (a statue shaped like a little TV antenna). In his acceptance speech, he joked to his fellow broadcast dignitaries, who included FOX executives: "Oh, great, now I can get FOX."

Our ratings, by the end of the season, slowly rose to the point where we ended up as the 111th show out of 125. It was a far cry from the hit we would eventually become, but in the embryonic FOX universe, it was enough to get us picked up for the second season. Also heartening was the growing word of mouth. We would get letters from fans who would say, "We love the Bundys.

They're just like us." "I have an uncle who is just like Al." Ed and Katey said people on the street would thank them for showing what family life is really like and some men would assume Al's plaintive pose and imitate his signature move—sticking their hand down their pants.

Gerry Cohen recalls being buoyed by a letter we received from a man in Pittsburgh that proved that our attack on traditional sitcoms was resonating:

> *Gentlemen,*
>
> *I have been a loyal fan of your show, "Married with Children," and I must say that I have thoroughly enjoyed each episode. Most shows on TV these days are simply unrealistic and downright false. For me, watching your show is a well needed break to the end of each week. I have a job I don't care for, a wife that doesn't seem to love me as much as I would want. I have two kids that don't give a damn whether I'm coming or going, and as bad as any given week in my life is, I know that on Sunday nights I can turn on the TV and see that Al Bundy's is even worse. I am writing to you in hopes you understand how important this show is to many viewers like me. Keep up the good work and thanks for keeping Al miserable.*

Though most of the first bumpy season exploited the contentious relationship between the Bundys and the Rhoadeses, our final episode, "Johnny B. Gone," focused on the Bundy nuclear family and the plight of Al, a reluctant but committed family man.

Al and Peggy's repeated attempts to get to an event commemorating the closing of a sentimental hamburger joint where they first met and courted when they were young and carefree—Johnny B. Goode's—are stifled by their children's high dramas. As Al and Peggy are first getting ready to leave, Kelly enters in hysterics. Her *life is over* because she wasn't invited to the big party tonight that everyone else is going to. Al, anxious to make it to the restaurant event before it closes, hurriedly imparts to her the wisdom of what he did at her age.

> **AL:** Just show up anyway. The important thing is— you wanna be there, be there. Even if they hate you. You're a Bundy! Start acting like one!

Almost out the door, Al is then waylaid by Bud who insists Dad fix his remote control car as promised for the big race event he's attending with his friends tonight. By the time Al gets the car running, though, he and Peggy have missed the Johnny B. Goode party and the opportunity to have a fun time with their friends and say a final farewell to what appeared to be a way happier era in their lives.

On a traditional sitcom, this would be when the parents would realize that sacrificing their own needs for their kids was the most important thing and a hug and the strains of the theme song would play us out of the episode. Instead, Al is resentful and poses the series defining question:

> **Al:** Never wanted to get married—I'm married. Never wanted to have kids—I got two of 'em. How the hell did this happen?

However, once Al has purged his emotions, he and Peggy are able to reflect on what just happened and, in their own Bundy way let us know how strong their bond really is and, thus, in the fittingly final lines of the first season they give us a little peek behind the curtain, into just how the hell it did happen.

PEGGY: Yeah, we just missed the end of an era.

AL: Yep.

Al and Peggy walk over to the couch.

AL: Well, we'll start a new era.

PEGGY: How? We don't have any traditions, we're Bundys.

AL: We still have one tradition. Remember what we used to do when we came back from Johnny B. Goode's?

PEGGY: Ah ha ha, in my parents' living room?

AL: Yeah.

Al and Peggy sit down on the couch. Al picks up the TV remote control and switches on the TV.

Al puts his arm over Peggy's shoulder, they watch TV, and smile.

Which is as close to a traditional sitcom Golden Moment as the show will ever come.

POSTSCRIPT—AL ENTERS FROM WORK

In a sitcom, when a main character enters a scene that's already in progress, it pulls the focus from whatever else is happening at the moment and provides the opportunity to get a quick character joke and also to set up the action of what's going to happen next. For example, every time Norm enters the Cheers bar and grunts some variation of, "It's a dog-eat-dog-world and I'm wearing Milk-Bone underwear," you're happy to see your old friend Norm, you know exactly what his current state of mind is, and you're curious about whatever adventures are about to unfold in the place "where everybody knows your name." Similarly, when Kramer crash-slides into Seinfeld's apartment, he is abrupt, unapologetic, and quick to join in with whatever Jerry is up to.

Married's take on the entrance joke was for Al to enter his front door in a world-weary fashion, reminding us that, for him, coming home will be no solace from the hell he just left at shoe store. In Season 1, the very first time we used this kind of entrance, Al walks in and simply throws away the line:

> **AL:** Feet and the return of warm weather sure makes for a deadly combination.

In another early episode, when Al enters and Peggy asks him how his day was, he spikes the ball a little more:

> **AL:** I sell shoes, okay? Geez, it stinks in here. Oh well. What's for dinner?

Encouraged by the audience response to these jokes and how well it suited Al, we started to broaden and exaggerate them, often to the point of absurdity and the outer edge of decency.

AL: A fat woman came into the shoe store today and said that she was a size five. I shoved her hoof into a shoe, my thumb got stuck in the back of the shoe. She panicked, reared up, and galloped around the store, dragging me on the floor behind her. Thank God a stick of butter popped out of her purse, so I was able to grease my way out of there.

Clearly these jokes would never fly today, given the greater sensitivity to making fun of weight and appearance, but Leavitt and Moye always tried to make sure that, in these instances, Al was firing back instead of throwing the first punch. "It cannot be enjoyable for you," Ron and Michael cautioned Ed. "In other words," O'Neill, explained, "if I was just in there making insults, on some level, that character would be enjoying doing that just for the heck of it. That was never the way they designed the show. Al was always put-upon. He was badgered. He was pushed around. It was always—'This doesn't fit me; what's wrong with *you*, Al Bundy?!'"

Mixing it up a little, in the spirit of keeping the audience ahead of what we know will be a huge insult, Peggy gives viewers a wink of acknowledgment during this entrance.

AL: I wish the world were a fly and I was a giant rolled-up newspaper.

PEGGY: Here we go.

AL: A fat woman clip-clopped into the shoe store today…and said, "I need something I'd be comfortable in." I said, "Try Wyoming."

Just to show that we're good sports and can be the target of our own satire, we turn around and mock Al's entrances by giving a similar one to a *put-upon* Kelly when she enters the house from her soul-sucking job as greeter at the TV Land Theme Park.

> **KELLY:** Why doesn't the world explode into a fiery, pus-filled death? A fat woman comes to the gate today, her muumuu covering what must've been three or four heinies. Now, she could exit through a little, itsy-bitsy turnstile or a huge gate. Guess which one she chooses. A line was forming. So I had to do something. So I got a tub of butter from the "Delta Burke, Let's Get Big" exhibit…and oiled her up. Then I went over to Star Trek Land, hot-wired the Enterprise, and sent it up where no man has gone before. She goes flying like a vegetable out of Dad's mouth…right into The Facts of Life Fan Club Pavilion. Thank G-d it's always empty. Can somebody give me a reason to live?

Then, Kelly sits down, sighs and slips her hand down her waistband and the transformation to her curmudgeonly father and our self-mocking bit is complete.

CHAPTER 7

SEASON 2: SANTA CLAUS DOWN!

THERE COULD HARDLY BE A more graphic example of FOX's original, disruptive, counterprograming strategy than early in Season 2, when *Married... With Children*'s first Christmas show ran head-to-head, at the exact same time and date on FOX, as *Family Ties*' Christmas episode ran on NBC. To understand why FOX put so much weight on this competitive tactic and how this particular evening aligned so perfectly with their goals, it's important to look at how different TV was back in 1989 versus today.

At the time, TV was strictly a linear universe. Though there was some video recording, it was well before today's viewer-friendly technology and streaming services allowed you to watch your favorite shows on you own schedule. Thus, you were essentially forced to watch first-run network shows on ABC, CBS, and NBC, only at the *exact* time in which they were broadcast.

"Counterprogramming was a full-time obsession for us," Ted Harbert recalls of his days as head of ABC. "We spent countless hours plotting which movie to put against their movies, where to schedule big specials and miniseries, using the competitive information supplied by a woman who worked for me and spent all day, every day *spying* on CBS and NBC."

The networks even created brands designed to lead you from one show to the next without being tempted to change channels. For example, NBC's Must See TV had the powerhouse lineup of *The Cosby Show*, leading off at 8 PM eastern, followed by *Family Ties*, at 8:30 then *Cheers* at 9, followed by *Night Court* at 10. ABC had TGIF, starting with *Perfect Strangers*, then *Family Matters* and then *Full House*, followed by *Step by Step*. To keep you even more hooked, they occasionally went so far as to create "theme nights" where the characters and stories overlapped. For example, one night was promoted as "TGIF Time Machine," in which Salem, from *Sabrina the Teenage Witch*, used Sabrina's powers to cause the characters in each of the other TGIF shows to travel back to different points in time, thus weaving the shows together.

FOX, even with its limited ratings success in its first season and factoring in that they were a new network was, therefore, sticking to the calculation that the only way to make a long-term dent into these deeply ingrained, hugely promoted, heavily branded, linear viewing habits was to provide something extremely different in the same time slot and hope the audience would be curious enough to switch the channel to FOX, or, as Barry Diller would say: "be dragged over by their shirt collar." This brings us to NBC's and FOX's dueling Christmas shows.

On *Family Ties*, Alex Keaton (Michael J. Fox) takes a job as a mall Santa for extra money, but he becomes so deeply moved when a little girl sits on his lap and wishes for "Santa" to bring her father home for the holidays that he invites her to join the Keatons for Christmas dinner. During the course of the evening, the girl's father "magically" shows up.

Meanwhile, over on *Married... With Children*, Al, Peg, Marcy, and Steve are on the couch watching live TV news coverage of a mall Santa whose publicity stunt—skydiving into the local mall on Christmas Day—goes horribly awry when, while he's holding a bottle of booze in each hand, his parachute fails to open and he crash lands into the Bundy backyard and dies a brutal death, in full view of the family (and the audience). A slightly different Christmas miracle than *Family Ties'* bringing Daddy home for the holidays.

"That was the Christmas episode in which we almost lost it on air," David Garrison recalls vividly. "Santa Claus's parachute doesn't work and you see Santa Claus falling and you hear the awful noise, and we all turn around, slowly, and right at the end, you can see us start to go. Just lost it. Funny stuff." Ed O'Neill had a similar reaction: "I could hear him (Santa Claus) cracking through the trees and, you know, I lost it. It was the only time I ever lost it on the stage. It was one of the funniest things I've ever seen." This "inappropriate laughing" phenomenon happens enough times during filming that there is even a term for it, *corpsing*, so-named because the worst time to have the giggles is when one is playing a corpse or, in this case, watching Santa Claus *become* a corpse.

As if killing Santa wasn't shocking enough, moments later the neighborhood kids who witnessed the fall, rush to the Bundy door to see if Old Saint Nick is okay. A reluctant Al dons dead Santa's costume and greets the kids to assure them that all is well. When one kid asks Santa to bring him a pony for Christmas, we see yet another difference between *Family Ties* and *Married...*

With Children's episodes, as Al delivers his version of giving a hopeful kid a Christmas Wish.

> **AL:** Your mom's the one who makes the pies for everyone in the neighborhood except those nice Bundys. Okay, Santa will leave you a pony under your tree. But if it isn't there in the morning, that means your mommy chased it away and killed it.

Then Al grants a *wish* to another kid, Nestor, whose mother also speaks ill of Al.

> **AL:** Here's a special gift for you: tell your dad to come home around the time when Mr. Mailman has a special delivery for Mommy. That'll be a real yuletide treat for Dad.
>
> **NESTOR:** What do I get?
>
> **AL:** A new home, and a fresh new mommy.

We even satirized parental guidance warnings when we posted a card ahead of that episode that read: "The following depicts a Bundy Christmas. It could be upsetting to small children and others. Parental guidance is suggested." Tipper Gore would be proud.

Our yuletide spoof turned out so well, we took a similar slam this season at traditional Valentine's Day shows, with an "interactive" feature, where the home audience could vote as to whether, at the end of the show, Al would grant Peggy her wish and say: "I love you," for her Valentine's present. We shot the finale both ways and when 67 percent of the audience voted "yes," we rolled the "I love you," version.

> **AL:** All right, Peg, I'm going to say it. But before I say it, I want to tell you I really hate you for this. I don't want to do it. I'm unhappy. My stomach is boiling, my palms are sweating. And if you think you're gonna get a jump after this, you're sadly mistaken! Of course, if you had a brain in that huge head, you'd know how I feel. But, you wanna hear it, fine. This is what you want, it's your stinkin' lousy Valentine's Day present. So here it is: (PAUSES) I love you.

After all of that, Peggy got the biggest laugh and totally made the moment work with her reading of:

> **PEGGY:** (THRILLED) Oh, Al! You didn't have to say that!

"Ron and I might have created the character of Peggy Bundy," Michael recalls, "but it was Katey who created the *persona*. Originally, we saw Peggy as much more frumpy, your stereotypical hausfrau, but Katey gave her the leggings, the wig, the *life* which even today causes most men to ask themselves, 'Why wouldn't Al want to sleep with her?' Without what Katey gave to the character, we would've had a much more mundane, gray, lifeless series."

Al and Peggy's thorny sex life was a go-to topic both for jokes and to satirize family comedies, like *Happy Days* where Howard would came home at noon to get "frisky" with Marion, or when Samantha constantly "bewitches" Darrin. "The sexual wrinkle worked," said O'Neill. "We started talking about how sexual bliss was not exactly part of our marriage, and that was like a bomb that went off around the country—the fact that a husband and wife might not find each other wildly exciting after a number of years. We not only talked about it, we had fun with it. And I think a lot of people in their living rooms were going, 'Yeah, that's how it really is' or 'Thank God, someone is worse off than we are.'" We also made sure the jokes weren't all just on Peggy.

> **PEGGY:** Which brings us to a little promise you made, just last spring.
>
> **AL:** Sex again. Peg, we've been married for seventeen years now, can't we just be friends?
>
> **PEGGY:** No. I don't like you; I just want to have sex with you!

Not only did Al and Peggy have fun with it, by Season 2, they also toyed with Steve and Marcy, who reveled in their sexual attraction. In "The Razor's Edge," for example, when Steve returns from a solo camping trip with a full beard and horny as hell, Marcy is so repulsed, she refuses to have sex with him until he shaves it off. Steve, with Al's "helpful support," makes a stand and refuses to shave. Days later, however, when Steve, now kicked out of his house and sleeping on the Bundys' couch, becomes so horny he's about to break, Al rolls out the big guns and delivers a classic *Married... With Children* moment.

> **AL:** Steve, I'm going to give you a gift. A special gift to make you stop thinking about Marcy. I didn't want to do this until it was absolutely necessary, so sit down.

Clear your mind. Think of Marcy. Now, take a look at this photo of...my mother-in-law (SHOVES A PHOTO AT HIM).

STEVE: AHHHHHHHHHH!

AL: Everybody says that. Yep, look at her in a two-piece bathing suit, bending over at the beach on the shore of Lake Michigan to pick up her sunglasses, the summer of '71. Notice the perspiration percolating in the folds of her stomach. You'll also notice that her upper arms are blurry. Why you ask? Well, there was a breeze and the camera caught them in mid-flap.

This kills the urge for Steve until Marcy, inspired by Peggy, walks in and flashes open her coat to reveal she is wearing nothing but a sexy lingerie ensemble, which immediately breaks Steve's will and resets the relationship as they run home to shave and have sex.

Though mother-in-law jokes have been a staple of sitcoms forever, our *cold shower* twist on it got such a huge reaction it became a signature sequence. It is always shown on a highlight reel to our live audiences before the show to get them in the *Married... With Children* mood and it is always included in links to the "The Best of Al Bundy" clips on YouTube and other fan sites.

David Garrison, in referring to this scene, made a comment that counters, or at least questions the view that *Married... With Children* always glorified men at the expense of women: "It's interesting that a show conceived by men would have such powerful women in the two households and the men were always bouncing off these women in random ways that are confusing to the men and frustrating to them and ultimately educates them but it's the women who have the power."

As we continued to watch how our live audiences responded to our characters and plot lines in Season 2, we learned a lot about writing those characters. Primarily, we saw that the Bundy-Rhoades rivalry was still our primary story engine for the audience's enjoyment, but we also observed how strongly David and Christina were stepping into their Bud and Kelly roles. This inspired us to give them some more screen time, expanding their characters in ways designed to underscore the dysfunctional family premise. They could antagonize each other as well as drive their parents insane.

> **BUD:** This is going to be my special day. Any girls call me?
>
> **KELLY:** Yep, they call you "geek," "dork," "hairy palms."

Bud may have been the butt of Kelly's jokes about his awkwardness with girls, but he had some cards of his own to play regarding his sister's rather obvious deficits in other areas. In one episode, a bewildered Kelly comes to Bud for help on her book report on *Robinson Crusoe*. He cons her into thinking it's the story of *Gilligan's Island* and if she simply copies the following lyrics and sings this song she'll get an "A" on her report.

KELLY WRITES FURIOUSLY AS BUD SINGS, TO THE TUNE OF THE *GILLIGAN'S ISLAND* THEME SONG

BUD: Just sit right back and you'll hear a tale,
A tale of a fateful trip.
That started from this tropic
port aboard this tiny ship.
The mate—That's Robinson—
was a mighty sailing man,
The skipper brave and sure.
Five passengers set sail that day
for a three-hour tour…
A *three*-hour tour.

We brought this bit back later when Bud convinces Kelly that Poe's "The Raven" is actually *The Adams Family*.

BUD: De, Duh, Duh, Dum (SNAP, SNAP)
De Duh Duh Dum, (SNAP, SNAP)
The Ra-ven Fam-ily.

In yet other episode, Bud takes advantage of Kelly's naivete when he tells her that Melville's classic, *Moby Dick*, was the story of a talking whale named Wilbur.

BUD: A whale is a whale
Of course, of course.
And no one's talked to a whale
Of course.
Unless, of course
The whale, of course.
Is the fabulous Mr. Dick.

Though the actors by this point in the second season were getting accustomed to the rhythm of shooting shows in front of a live audience, and though we loved working that way, Ed O'Neill was having a hard time with the process whereby we (the writers) would make line changes to the actors' lines between "takes" in the middle of live shows. These writing changes were prompted by the audience's response—or lack thereof—to the dialogue the actors had just delivered with the hope of getting a bigger laugh.

"I was used to the theater and movies," Ed explained, "and I always liked knowing my lines, because there's an insecurity about not knowing them. So, when we're doing those in front of the live audience, sometimes there's rewriting going on, which I appreciated and didn't like at the same time. Because, early on, I was insecure about going up and flubbing a line. I said, 'I don't know this damn line.' I don't know the change, and now I've got to switch over to this new line in midstream, and, often times, I would make a mistake and I would always show that I wasn't happy. And too many times the audience would see it.

"So, one time after a show, I was going home, and my wife was in the car with me and I was saying, 'Motherfucker, I couldn't remember those new lines that they wrote.' She said, 'Why do you get mad? You're going to make a mistake when you don't know it. You're not a machine and the audience doesn't like it when you get mad. They like it when you *don't* get mad. When you make a mistake, you can make a joke, or you can laugh at yourself. The audience enjoys that.'

"She was right," Ed acknowledged. "From that point on I was pretty much over that. I started saying, 'All right, you go up, have fun with it, because it's gonna happen, and if you know its gonna happen, it'll take a little stress off you."

Also in Season 2, predating episodes that play on Al's well-known obsession with strip clubs, is an episode where Peggy and her friends go to Troy's, a male strip club. In the first of two very well-travelled sitcom joke roads, Peggy swears she's never been to a strip club before, which was a bald setup for a joke where she walked into the club, was greeted by name, and was asked if she wanted her usual table. In a similar traditional sitcom joke pattern, the moment after Marcy swears that putting a dollar bill down a stripper's G-string is immoral, we flip to Marcy shamelessly shoving a fist full of dollars deep into the crotch of a stripper named Zorro.

The Troy's episode also sets up a *Married* parody of still another sitcom trope in which a character loses their wedding or engagement ring and is desperate to get it back before their partner discovers it's lost. On NBC's *Friends*, Rachel loses hers in Monica's lasagna. On ABC's *Home Improvement*, Tim accidentally knocks Jill's wedding ring into the drain. On *Married… With Children,* wouldn't you know it, Marcy loses her ring down Zorro's pants while stuffing dollars in there and eventually has to deal with Steve finding out how in the world that happened. Ted Harbert, whose network broadcast *Home Improvement*, recalls that Marcy losing her ring down a stripper's crotch versus Jill Taylor losing hers down the kitchen drain generated a lot of envy and complaints to the higher-ups that ABC wasn't allowed to be that bold. His broadcast standards and sales departments, however, still held the line that FOX was gleefully dancing across.

While *Married* may have been guilty of perpetuating the stereotype that female strippers are not the brightest bulbs in the box, we discovered while casting this episode that male strippers might just fit the stereotype even better. Our casting director at the time, Tammi Billick, remembers going to Chippendale's for the first phase of the casting for the "Girls Just Want to Have Fun" strip show episodes and making her initial choices strictly on how the male strippers looked and danced and then bringing the best ones back to Michael and Ron and the rest of us for the final casting decisions. One of the dancers who was obviously not an experienced actor, was reading not only *his* lines but the stage directions (action lines) as if they were dialogue. So it was: "*Hi, Peggy.* (READS STAGE DIRECTION) *He turns to look at Peggy. I am Igor.* (READS STAGE DIRECTION) *He sits down on the chair.*" We told him, "You're not supposed to read the stage directions *out loud.*"

So the next take was: "*Hi Peggy* (WHISPERS STAGE DIRECTION) *He turns to look at Peggy. I am Igor.* (WHISPERS STAGE DIRECTION) *He sits down on the chair.*" As talented he was at being a male stripper, he simply did not have the acting chops to get the part.

By the middle of the second season, tensions between FOX and the show had calmed down a little from the conflicts that had surrounded the pilot and the first few episodes. FOX, to its credit, was keeping its promise of not interfering with or censoring us. We even got a bit cocky, making the network the butt of some biting jokes regarding their programming vulnerabilities. When the Bundys are watching TV, and we hear:

TV ANNOUNCER: And I'd like to say one more time please, *please* watch *The Late Show* on FOX. All we want is a chance. Is that too much to ask for?

Based on the dismal ratings for *The Late Show*, despite the shuffling of hosts from Joan Rivers to Buck Henry to Arsenio Hall, apparently it was.

With all the sophisticated ratings technologies employed by the networks, exhaustively parsing demographics, household spending, sleeping habits, and the like, Michael Moye recalls his *seat-of-the-pants* barometer for *Married*'s success when he observed the audience's reaction to the two-part episode that opened our second season. "It was the first time I can recall that we were actually making an impact with the audience.

"We did a show called, 'Poppy's by the Tree,' where Al and Peggy took their very, very low-budget vacation to a backwater town in Florida, where a serial killer was on the loose and targeting the Bundys. It was a spoof on horror movies and I was very surprised that it didn't get, as we were taping it, the audience reaction, the pop that we were used to. I wasn't sure why, because I thought—well, it was just as funny as the other shows.

"We figured it out: the audience did not like to see the Bundy characters in jeopardy. They cared about them so much that even in a spoof where they could possibly be harmed, it really turned the audience off. At that point, we knew we really had something. Because that's what you want. You want the audience to care about these characters without going, 'Baby, you're the greatest'—just let them grow on you."

Though Michael and Ron did not set out to create a ratings smash, and were driven by their gut instincts rather than sophisticated tracking charts, we were fully aware that the *alternative* FOX Network was still driven by *traditional* standards of success, so we were encouraged by the slight uptick in the year's final numbers, from a basically incalculable rating in Season 1 to a low, but nonetheless measurable 4.7 by the close of Season 2. As we looked forward to the upcoming Season 3, however, we had no idea that a force worse than bad ratings was waiting in the wings—a force that threatened to kill us and take FOX down in the process.

POSTSCRIPT—MARCY RANTS

Season Two also gave birth to the phenomenon of, "Marcy rants" in which the tightly wound banker suddenly gets triggered and erupts like a bubbling geyser. For example, when somebody mentions Elvis,

> **MARCY:** I saw him in Vegas. His buns alive with magic. His voice pulsing through me reaching my secret places. His hips undulating, swirling, grinding, driving his essence into my very soul again and again. Faster and faster until…until…(HAS A TREMBLING, ONSTAGE ORGASM, THEN) Can I have a cigarette?

"Ed gave me the idea to keep the orgasm primarily a mental experience," Amanda recalled. "Great choice. Evidently, I had a good time. But trust me, that was a performance."

"We wanted to show," Michael said, "she wasn't the perfect and delicate wallflower that she initially presented herself as and behind the facade of the straight-laced, buttoned-down, conservative elitist, she was a little unsure of who she was herself," as when in another episode she said:

> **MARCY:** I love to go to the dentist! A man in white hovering over me while I'm trapped helpless in a chair. He cleans me, he flosses me, his instrument's alive in my mouth. And just when I think I can't take any more he says, "Good girl, Marcy. You can spit now." (SMILES AND WIPES HER CHIN)

Which sets Peggy up, as she replies:

> **PEGGY:** Al, I want to go to the dentist.

"I always appreciated when more dimensionality was explored in the storytelling," Amanda said. "I think Marcy was more complicated than what the Bundys saw or thought of her." Another totally spontaneous eruption comes in Season 7's "Frat Chance," when Marcy cautions Bud about the perils of joining a fraternity.

> **MARCY:** Don't you think I know anything about fraternities? Desperate girls, coming from everywhere, trying anything to land a college man before he becomes successful and realizes he can get a much better and bustier girl. Not that it wasn't fun for me. Doing anything with anybody. My once-demure dress lying ripped and forgotten. As forgotten as I was when the sun came up. Jim, you bastard! Why don't you return my calls?! (THEN, CALM) That was just a composite of other women's stories.

After several of these multilayered fantasies, Marcy shares her version of what she considers a *simple* one.

MARCY: I like to keep my fantasies simple. It starts with me in a really tight, short dress at the end of a bar. At the other end, they're greasing up Mike Tyson. He's shadowboxing and starting to sweat. Then the scene changes. It's now Madison Square Garden. A smoky crowd throbs with anticipation. 'Go, Marcy,' they buzz. Tyson turns into George Forman, who eyes me like a basket of muffins. The bell rings. I try to fight but I'm powerless. Then our eyes meet. He gives me the old one-two. The crowd is on its feet cheering. I'm down. The count starts. The crowd's screaming, 'Get up,' but I can't. I won't! Take me, Mandingo!

ade against *Married… With Children* that got so much traction
threatened to get our show cancelled and bring the network
wn with us.

"I can remember going to the office, having to get into the
vator to go to the third floor," Michael Moye recalls about
first awareness of the Rakolta story. "It was a slow, creak-
elevator. I kinda use this elevator every morning as a meta-
, because it would take me from the ground floor reality of
Angeles up three flights into the *Married… With Children*
s. By that time, I would almost always hear bad news com-
f the elevator.

ut that day, as it happened, was going to be a good day.
e, I remembered, that day we were going to be casting
layboy Playmates so, of course, the elevator was going
han usual. And by the time I got to the third floor it
Playboy Playmate standing there, it was my assistant,
lling me: 'Did you hear the news that someone called
lained about the show that aired last night and they
unhappy?' My response was, 'That's too bad, where are
tes? And she said, 'No, they're taking this seriously.' I
is taking this seriously?' She said, '*Everyone* is taking
y.'"

rted the night before when Terry Rakolta who, by
unt, was simply looking to watch something "fam-
on TV with her kids, aged seven, eight, and nine.
the Michigan mother to turn on an episode of
ith Children" called "Her Cups Runneth Over,"
the following: in the first scene, we discover it's
y and she jokes about how this year she wants Al
ething different, "something that lasts over three

CHAPTER 8

SEASON 3: TERRYIED… WITH CHILDREN—PART 1

SEASON 3 OF *MARRIED… WITH Children* was to the family sitcom what *The Godfather Trilogy* was to the gangster film, except
Married had more senseless violence, gratuitous sex, and a less
sympathetic family.

The blood starting flowing early on *Married* when we shot
what was supposed to be our third season (1998–1999) opening
episode, "A Period Piece." The period in question was a shared
menstrual cycle—Peggy, Kelly, and Marcy—which came, as fate
and sitcom traditions would have it, at the worst possible time.
Not only did it disrupt a temporary truce among the usually
hostile neighbors who had decided to share a weekend vacation
together in a one-room cabin in the wilderness, it triggered pri-
mal instincts in wild animals that surrounded the cabin, trap-
ping the families in. Given the many permutations of combative
dyads stuck in that room, it was hard to know whether it was
more life-threatening to be inside or outside the cabin, which
was exactly what we were going for.

Thus, *Married… With Children* tapped into one of the oldest sitcom tropes in television—"the lock-in show"—a device for
characters who are otherwise at odds to bond in their entrapped

predicament and become more empathetic to their fellow trapped victims, only to return to being rivals the next week. A classic example was an *All in the Family* episode where Archie and his son-in-law Mike (aka Meathead) get trapped in a basement and Mike gains empathy for Archie when he learns that Archie's father used to hit him when he was a kid and lock him in the closet. Or on *Family Ties*, when Mallory and Skippy get locked in a basement and find that, in spite of their vast differences, they have something in common—they're both idiots.

In *Married... With Children*'s version of the trapped show, "We weren't in this to teach little girls anything, or enlighten our characters," according to Michael Moye. "We just wanted to make Al's life miserable." That said, Michael might have been selling the episode's educational value short. The National Park Service concluded in their "Study on Bears and Menstruating Women" that: "free-ranging bears detected and consumed used tampons, but ignored nonmenstrual human blood and unused tampons." The study was written "so that women can make an informed choice when deciding whether or not to hike and/or camp in bear country during their menstrual period."

Though FOX's censors never questioned the "bear-tampon hypothesis" or gave us credit for advancing it, they were very concerned about the graphic subject matter of the episode. "I guess they didn't feel the idea of menstruation," Moye surmised, "was appropriate. This episode was written by Marci Vosburgh and Sandy Sprung, a female writing team on our staff. All the network notes came from men. 'You want to argue about this,'" Moye told FOX at the time, "argue with Marcy and Sandy. Tell them that the notion that they menstruate is inappropriate, ew, ew, ew…tell them."

Amanda Bearse remembers: "…getting the gi the shooting of 'A Period Piece.' Katey, Chrissy lying on the floor and couldn't say our lines with Unfortunately, the network was not similarly am down hard on the show, demanding significant of all the network's bluster, we ended up cha lines, like we always did. Even with these r FOX was still so skittish about the subject m it demanded we change the title from, "A P Camping Show." In the end, *title cleansing* calm the choppy waters this show stirred

"A Period Piece" was originally sche opener, an episode traditionally desigr showcase that resets the tone of the s ers back into the fold and attract ne Therefore, the network puts a lot r promoting it, attaching catchy slog *the Year*," and "*This is FOX*." It ha of sorts and often gets reviewed a

For all these reasons, FOX Piece," even retitled as "The C opener. Instead, it chose to ru figured it wouldn't get as m figure, however, was that l *Children* would gain more a real-life plot twist more had ever cooked up in r a protective mother fr single episode of our s

minutes." Then we learn that Peggy is bent out of shape (literally and figuratively) because the manufacturer of her favorite bra has discontinued making it and, though she's shopped around, no other bra fits as well as her old model. This leads to a vibrator joke and also to Rakolta sending her kids out of the room while she continued to watch the show in disbelief.

At this point in the story, Steve convinces Al that the only place that's likely to still have a supply of Peggy's discontinued bra is Francine's of Hollywood, a lingerie store in Oconomowoc, Wisconsin, which is hundreds of miles from Chicago. Al is so desperate to please his distressed wife because, as he put it—

> **AL:** They discontinued my wife's bra, yet my wife lives on.

—he agrees to go on a quest there with Steve to buy Peggy the only bra that will make her happy.

Once Al and Steve make their trek from Chicago to Wisconsin, they enter Francine's, modeled after the trashy Frederick's of Hollywood, where we see with a parade of models and customers wandering about in revealing lingerie. "I'm shocked," Rakolta told me. "Seeing that in my living room and *not* choosing it. I thought it was porn." Terry then gave this very detailed and, for the most part, accurate account of the rest of the show.

- They had a man in the store wearing a garter belt and nylons.
- Steve "childishly" twirls the pasties on a nude mannequin's breasts. (Not sure there's a mature way to do this).

- They had a man watching porno movies walking around, bent over, with an erection. (The man is Steve, and though he is clearly bent over, no arousal is apparent).

- A saleswoman assumes that Al and Steve are a gay couple shopping together but Al sets her (and Steve) straight: **AL:** And if I was gay, I'd like to think I could do better than him.

- A young woman with her back to the camera asks Al "if her boyfriend would like her better with or without the bra," which she removes (covering her breasts with her hands, though she is still showing some "side boob"), causing Al to faint on the floor.

- Meanwhile back at the Bundy house, a male stripper, who is a birthday present from Marcy to Peggy, strips down to a G-string in front of the delighted women.

"I looked to see," Rakolta remembers, "who was doing the advertising—oil-change shops or cigarettes—and I saw it was American Airlines, Kentucky Fried Chicken, Coca-Cola, Tambrands…allegedly family-friendly companies. I went to bed that night and I was lying there thinking, why would companies like this be promoting lifestyles like that and putting it into family viewing hours? It was the infringement into my living room during the Family Hour."

The next day, an incensed Rakolta started a letter-writing campaign, shooting off twenty missives to the show's advertisers, citing the above examples, accusing the sponsors of "pandering to and supporting soft core pornography." She concluded with what might just as well have been the mission statement of the Family Viewing Hour: "It's 8:30 Sunday evening. How come this is coming into my living room?"

"My problem wasn't really the show itself," she told me. "I wouldn't have cared if it was after 9 PM. *We* have the Family Viewing Hour. *You* take it from 9 o'clock on. Show what you want. Who cares?"

Not content to simply fire off letters, Rakolta decided to call FOX and personally protest the show. But because FOX was so small at the time, it didn't have a department to officially handle complaints so, unbeknownst to Rakolta, her call got routed from their switchboard to our production office where Marcy Vosburgh, the cowriter of the episode in question, was told to take the call. Rakolta thought she was speaking to someone at FOX and Vosburgh had no clue exactly what was going on.

"I answered the phone," Vosburgh recalled, "and there was this woman saying, 'I saw your show last night and it was absolutely offensive." Vosburgh's first approach was to confess that her own mother didn't like the show but that we were just, "trying something new." When this didn't mollify Rakolta, Vosburgh suggested that if she felt the show was so insulting she had the freedom to simply, "stand up, walk to the television and change the channel." This only made Rakolta angrier and confirmed that she had to go further and take personal action.

I asked Rakolta if she would have reacted differently had she known at the time she had been talking to the writer of the episode rather than a FOX executive. She said she would have and, "If she (Vosburgh) just would have said, 'I'm sorry. You have a couple of points here. I'll talk to the producers and bring that

up,' even if she would have lied, I would have been satisfied."
We'll never know for sure but we do know that when Rakolta
heard Marcy say, "My only recourse was to change the channel,
I was so mad. It was like, 'Game on.' We'll see how far we can
take this."

Rakolta immediately reached out to the sponsors she
had already written to, including Coca-Cola, Kimberly-
Clark, Mitsubishi, Wendy's, Tambrands, Johnson & Johnson,
McDonald's, and Proctor & Gamble. Now she upped the ante
considerably, threatening: "If you indeed support this type of
programming message, I will be obligated to take the next step,
and start a boycott of all your products."

Rakolta's campaign soon mushroomed into a media feeding
frenzy that broke on the front page of the *New York Times*, followed by TV interviews on *Larry King Live*, ABC's *Nightline*, and
all the morning TV talk shows, culminating in a major sponsor
boycott that threatened to derail both the show and the fledgling
FOX network. "I woke up in bed with my husband," Rakolta
recalls, "and all of a sudden at 6 o'clock in the morning all the
news shows are calling. *Oprah*, *Nightline*, everybody's calling. A
reporter called and said, 'Your picture is on the cover of the *New
York Times*.' I thought, *My husband has a high profile*. 'Are you
going to jail,' I asked? He said, 'No, it's *your* picture on there.'
I said, 'Am *I* going to jail?' Then it just kept going. I got death
threats. I had the FBI at the house."

"At first," Moye said, "it pretty much amused me because
here was one woman's opinion and, suddenly, it was on the front
page of the *New York Times*. I mean, did anybody kill anybody in
Lebanon today? *This* is the best you can do for the front page?"

One of the reasons Rakolta's tirade resonated so strongly was that she framed it in the context of the "Family Viewing Hour," a sacrosanct broadcast policy that started in 1977 when the FCC issued an edict that networks devote the hours of 8 to 9 PM Monday through Saturday and 7 to 9 PM on Sunday to feature light, family-appropriate fare, like *Full House*, *Growing Pains*, and so on. The policy was eventually ruled unconstitutional as a law, but as a practice, the code was strictly adhered to by the Big Three networks and taken as gospel by the advertising community and the home audience at large.

FOX, however, didn't have enough audience coverage at that time to *officially* qualify it as a *network*, so they were not *technically* bound by their codes, legal or otherwise. FOX took even more liberties with this technicality and decided to exploit this loophole to execute its counter-programming strategy and scheduled *Married... With Children* in the heart of the Family Viewing Hour—8 PM during its first season and 8:30 for two seasons after, hoping to attract new viewers. What it didn't count on was that Terry Rakolta would be one of those viewers.

The fallout was swift and strong. Shots in the culture wars were fired from predictable sides. Jesse Helms, the ultraconservative senator from North Carolina, who had previously called *Married... With Children*, "trash," extolled Rakolta's virtues on the floor of the U.S. Senate. *Hustler Magazine,* parodying *Penthouse Magazine's* Pet of the Month, dubbed Rakolta, Asshole of the Month. She was also called "The Ayatollah Rakolta." Rakolta felt the worst attack from the press, however, was that on Mother's Day, her "sealed" divorce papers were printed on the front page of the *Detroit News*.

Meanwhile, the show and the network were getting pummeled by some of the biggest businesses and advertisers in the world. The president of Coca-Cola, Ira C. Herbert, personally apologized to Rakolta, saying: "I am corporately, professionally, and personally embarrassed that one of our commercials appeared in this particularly unsuitable program episode."

Proctor & Gamble cancelled further advertising on *Married* "…due to its negative portrayal of the American family."

Kimberly-Clark took "action" after reviewing the "offending" episode.

After three seasons moving forward the monumental task of launching a new network, FOX was now backed into a corner—it either had to ride out the storm of controversy or abandon ship and cancel *Married… With Children*. It's important to note that even though *Married* was inching up in the ratings back then, it was still hanging on by a thread. Rob Kenneally, executive vice president of FOX, recalled that, at the time, "The future of the show was up in the air. *Married… With Children* could have stayed or gone. It did not have national awareness." It's also important to note that at that time in broadcast history, if you were cancelled, you were done. There were no cable or streaming services to fall back on and due to the nature of the series, there was no way ABC, NBC, or CBS would pick up the show on their traditional networks.

Rakolta remembers that "Jamie Kellner, [FOX Broadcasting president] called me personally. He apologized: 'Most of my writers haven't been further east than Aspen.' I didn't know what that means but we had a good talk. Nice guy. Just a difference of opinion."

Kellner's response to the media was: "Although *Married... With Children* stretches the limits of acceptable programming, its provocative scripts are merely a realistic depiction of lower middle class family values. Al Bundy is not supposed to be a sophisticated man who recognizes that women are equal to men." He likened the show to *All in the Family* and *Maude*, "which explored controversial issues in a humorous, yet trenchant way."

Rhetoric alone, however, was not going to fly in the face of this highly visible national controversy. Some extremely influential sponsors had already pulled out and FOX decided it had to make some significant moves or pack up its tent.

FOX's first offering was to say it would "look at the show's scripts more carefully" and make sure the producers "tone them down," an adjustment that was easy for them to offer as it would be hard to measure and play out only over a long period of time. The concession that turned out to be much more effective, however, and was clearly visible, came when FOX moved *Married... With Children*'s time slot from 8:30 to 9 PM, essentially honoring the Family Viewing Hour, one of Rakolta's key demands.

Soon thereafter, Coca-Cola, whose president was so, "personally embarrassed" by *Married... With Children*, ran more than twenty-five commercials for its products on the "unsuitable" show. Kimberly-Clark, which told Rakolta it had no further plans to advertise on the "offending" *Married... With Children*, started running ads for its Huggies brand diapers. Mitsubishi followed suit as did almost every other advertiser that had toadied up to the Michigan housewife, plus dozens of new advertisers that lined up to buy commercial time on the show...at now-inflated rates.

Lest you think these companies were convinced that *Married… With Children* and FOX were going to do a total 180-degree turn in the content department, or that moving to 9 PM insulated the show from family sensitivities, the real story was that all of the publicity Terry Rakolta brought to the show significantly boosted our ratings. Not just with total viewers but with the much coveted eighteen-to-thirty-four-year-old demographic—the gold standard for advertisers.

"The spike in our ratings," FOX executive Rob Kenneally recalls, "was so noticeable that we would get calls from press and/or peers in the industry saying, 'What a genius move,' thinking we had actually orchestrated it, which, of course, we hadn't. Everything she was trying to do actually backfired. People all of a sudden went to check it out. We wanted to put a bust of her in the lobby of the FOX network at one time."

Head of programming Garth Ancier added: "Terry Rakolta didn't realize she was actually helping us on multiple fronts: she was publicizing the show by vilifying it and she was helping us get more money for the commercials because the people who were pulling out as advertisers had the lowest rates."

Not only did the controversy attract new viewers to *Married*, but once they saw the series, they kept coming back week after week, making it the highest-rated show on FOX and, in some instances, beating its competition on the other networks. After the short-lived boycott, *Married… With Children* set an all-time television record by increasing its overall ratings by a whopping 117 percent.

The Rakolta incident "was a barometer that you were on the right track," according to TV critic Jackson Upperco. "It was like a rite of passage that you finally got someone to complain that the content wasn't what we were getting on *Family Ties* and the rest of the audience would say, 'Thank God' for that.' Today you would have had thousands of that woman on Twitter doing the same thing."

Rakolta soon faded from the headlines and stopped appearing on talk shows, but the "Rakolta Effect" was yet to die down and would still have a direct and negative impact on our show. Even though FOX and *Married* ultimately benefitted in popularity from the incident, there was still significant collateral damage to sort through on the ground. FOX's promise to look more closely at upcoming scripts was no mere lip service.

One casualty was FOX rejecting an idea for an episode where Al becomes "accidentally" circumcised (which we eventually shot, years later) but by far the biggest fallout was that FOX refused to air an entirely different show we had already shot for the current season and was soon scheduled to be broadcast—"I'll See You in Court." This episode, though no racier than any show we had shot before, was clearly a token gesture by FOX to the advertising community to make good on its other promise to "tone down" the series.

"I'll See You in Court" wasn't merely pushed to a later date, like FOX had done with "A Period Piece." FOX was so adamant about burying it, it was *never* broadcast on the network or anywhere else until thirteen years later when the entire *Married... With Children* series appeared on FOX's FX channel, was sold as a boxed DVD set, and also went into syndication on independent and cable outlets. In addition to this "Lost Episode" taking on a mythical status with fans and curiosity seekers alike, the banning of the episode reopened some of the wounds that were inflicted from the Rakolta ordeal and, as you will see, cast a giant shadow on the second half of the third season.

As a side note, the network tried to get us to fire Marcy Vosburgh, scapegoating her for stirring up an already outraged Terry Rakolta when she fielded her initial phone call. Ron and Michael, though they were accused by detractors of being immoral pornographers who were corrupting American values, as always were principled and stalwart in dealing with the people who did an honest job for them and refused to fire Marcy.

POSTSCRIPT—I WOULD RATHER

Season 3 also introduced Al's first signature "I would rather," response to a request he found so objectionable that his usual short, pithy comebacks didn't do it justice. For example, when Peggy suggested Al get a second job.

> **AL:** Peg, let me state this as clearly as I can. I would rather rip off my nose with a can opener. I would rather bob for apples in a sewer. I would rather have a catheter the size of a garden hose before I get another job to pay for your shopping.

Or, in "Buck Saves the Day," when Al is asked to take a group of young kids camping.

> **AL:** I would rather slam my nose in a car door. I'd rather have a proctologist named Dr. Hook. I'd rather watch Roseanne Barr do a striptease than take these little booger machines camping.

When Peggy suggested they have another child, Al had a slightly different idea.

AL: Gee, Peg, there's a couple of things I'd rather do first. Uh, I'd rather dive off the Sears Tower headfirst into a thumbtack. Or I'd rather bait a crocodile with my manhood. Which, I believe, is what got me into this mess.

Then, when they did have a child (which, as you will see, turned out to the product of a dream), and Peggy proposes their new addition sleep in their room, Al replies:

AL: I would like the record to show that I would rather sleep under a bunk bed with Oprah. I would rather engage in a frolicking threesome with Roseanne and her cool husband. I would rather play naked Twister with every one of the Golden Girls than to have that little screaming doodie geyser at the foot of my bed.

When anyone complained to Ed about being mean spirited, he always invoked what Jackie Gleason said to people who had similar problems with his character, Ralph Kramden, the gritty bus driver on *The Honeymooners*, "It was funny, that's what was so good about it. When you're doing a comedy it better be funny and we weren't trying to teach anybody anything."

CHAPTER 9

SEASON 3, CONTINUED: TERRYIED...WITH CHILDREN—PART 2

IN THE SEVENTY-PLUS-YEAR HISTORY OF network television, there have been many scripts that for one reason or another were summarily rejected by the network while still in the script stage, before they were even shot. There were also many shows originally broadcast in their regular time slot but due to extremely negative public response were never shown again on the original network. *Seinfeld*'s "The Puerto Rican Day," for example, created a backlash because viewers reacted negatively to Kramer accidentally lighting a Puerto Rican Flag on fire and stomping on it at the city's iconic Puerto Rican Day Parade. Due to public pressure, NBC never reran the episode again on its network, as it usually did, though it was broadcast four years later as part of the show's syndication package.

Star Trek's "Patterns of Force" featured Captain Kirk and crew donning Nazi uniforms to infiltrate a planet whose culture was based on Nazi Germany. It caused such an uproar it was never shown again, even though Kirk and the Federation were only using the costumes as a ruse to defeat the Nazis. Even a *Sesame*

Street episode was dumped after one viewing because parents said their kids were traumatized by the "scary witch."

There are, however, only a handful of episodes that were actually shot and *then* banned before they even aired. One of those rare instances was an episode of *Friends*, "The One Where Rachel Tells…" which was scheduled to air shortly after 9/11. It was never shown in its original form because it involved Chandler making a joke about a bomb while he was in an airport. NBC also decided not to air a *Fear Factor* it had shot called, "Hee Haw! Hee Haw!" that featured a challenge where two sets of twins each chugged a quart of donkey semen and urine.

Married… With Children joined this exclusive banned-before-broadcast club with Season 3's "I'll See You in Court," which we shot on January 6, 1989. Though it had been censored and rewritten in the script stage, the network and studio were still not satisfied with it after it was shot. "The timing couldn't have been worse," Michael Moye points out. "The Rakolta thing was still on the front burner and FOX went nuts." "I'll See You in Court" was ultimately banned and never broadcast on FOX. It was later dubbed "The Lost Episode," which has given it an aura of mystique.

The episode opens with Marcy convincing Peggy she'll get some much-needed bedroom action if she takes Al to an adult hotel frequented by the Rhoadeses, The Hop-On-Inn. Peggy cons Al into going and once they get into their room they watch an X-rated tape of a couple having wild sex. The Bundys are awestruck until they realize that the copulating couple is Steve and Marcy and then they become dumbstruck. Nonetheless, the Bundys end up having sex themselves.

Al and Peg get home and immediately taunt Steve and Marcy for having been tricked into doing a secret sex tape by the sleazy hotel. Al stops gloating, however, when Steve points out that the hotel must have also taped Al and Peggy having sex. Both couples, decide to sue the hotel for invasion of privacy.

In the courtroom, the jury first watches Exhibit A, the Rhoadeses' sex tape, which lasts a whopping four hours and three minutes and inspires a rousing ovation from the jury who awards them $10,000 for invasion of privacy. Then the jury watches, Exhibit B, the Bundy sex tape, which lasts only a few seconds, and they don't award the Bundys anything because they could find no evidence that a sexual act actually occurred.

Peggy, afraid that Al will lose whatever confidence he has in the sexual realm, pleads passionately to the court.

> **PEGGY:** Well, it may not be "sex" to you, but it is to me…Is a crumb not a banquet for a starving person? Is a fig leaf not clothing for the naked?

After the court is cleared, a humiliated Al has sex with Peggy right on the judge's bench, lasting for four hours and five minutes, getting a rousing ovation from the live audience. Peggy laments this sex act wasn't taped or it would have been worth a million dollars and we reveal the irony that the court's camera secretly recorded the entire act.

"The audience loved Al having sex with Peggy," according to O'Neill. "Ron Leavitt didn't want the audience to think that I couldn't get my hard on when I had to. Just like he always had me fighting bullies and gangs. Even if I got beat up, it was the *trying*, you know."

Though Season 3's "A Period Show," "Her Cups Runneth Over" and "I'll See You in Court" caused us the biggest headaches we had ever faced, according to critic, Jackson Upperco, "Season 3 was one of the best years, very formative and I see it as an uptick in the humor because all of the characters really have a perspective now and can help with stories. You still have the Steve and Marcy stuff going on but now you have other things to explore as well." This was particularly evident in "He Thought He Could," the episode that took the place of "A Period Piece" as Season 3's opener.

"He Thought He Could," was as edgy and satirical as our other episodes but it was a landmark for the series in the sense that there was no Bundy versus Rhoades, no Al versus Peggy, no sex or bodily functions to speak of. Instead, it tells a story that emphasizes "Al as everyman," who refuses to quit even in the face of the tremendous odds stacked against him.

Early in the episode we see a flashback of Al when he was nine years old (Edan Gross), already with the habit of sticking his hand down his waistband. Young Al is scorned by a contemptuous librarian, Miss DeGroot (Lu Leonard), who hates little "smartass Al" and curses his fate forever. As we shift to present time, Al is caught on video trying to sneak a copy of *The Little Engine That Could* he had checked out when he was nine, and which was now twenty-five years and $2,000 overdue, back into the library stacks without being noticed. Miss DeGroot, who still works there, catches Al in the act, however, and gloats that he grew up as she predicted, "a total and complete loser." Al responds in a stirring speech that has become one of the most iconic of the entire series.

AL: "So you think I'm a loser? Just because I have a stinking job that I hate, a family that doesn't respect me, a whole city that curses the day I was born? Well, that may mean loser to you, but let me tell you something. Every morning when I wake up, I know it's not going to get any better until I go back to sleep again. So I get up, have my watered-down Tang and still-frozen Pop-Tart, get in my car with no upholstery, no gas, and six more payments to fight traffic just for the privilege of putting cheap shoes on the cloven hooves of people like you. I'll never play football like I thought I would, I'll never know the touch of a beautiful woman, and I'll never again know the joy of driving without a bag on my head. But I'm not a loser. 'Cause despite it all, me and every other guy who'll never be what he wanted to be, are still out there, being what we don't wanna be, forty hours a week, for life. And the fact that I haven't put a gun to my mouth, you pudding of a woman, makes me a winner!"

Al's championing of the underdog appealed to viewers of all stripes and it also gave our live tapings the feel of a sporting event, amplified by the fact that we often had groups of L.A. Kings and L.A. Lakers players in our audience hooting and hollering at Al, sitting shoulder to shoulder with a crowd of fans who, ironically, were hooting and hollering at them on game nights.

With all deference to the writing it can't be stated strongly enough how convincingly Ed O'Neill played this everyman that his fans want crazy for. "Just about every defeated, downtrodden, moment during the series was brought to the table by Ed,"

Michael Moye said. "Sure, we wrote the jokes, but Ed's spin went just as far in making the humor."

Gerry Cohen added, "I don't think I ever had to say a single word to Ed about *who* Al Bundy is/was. Ed possessed an innate sense of how to exude a certain hopeless acceptance of Al's lot in life without it feeling bitter or angry in a way that would be off-putting to the audience. Kicked once again in the balls, he seemed to say, 'Is that the best ya got?' I think this is also why his small triumphs were so joyously celebrated by the audience."

In the same way, Katey Sagal, Christina Applegate, David Faustino, David Garrison, Amanda Bearse, and later Ted McGinley's artistic skill, likability, and fearless attack on decidedly unconventional characters were a big part of why we could not only get away with such provocative plot lines but began, in Season 3, to surge in the ratings.

Season 3 also saw a swell in the broad tone that had gradually been creeping into the show, foreshadowing an even bigger movement in this direction over the course of the rest of the series. For now, the broadness was still grounded in a semblance of reality, both in the lives of the characters and, as you will see, by no coincidence, their creators.

In the episode, "Eatin' Out," the Bundys decide to blow a small inheritance on an expensive family meal. When their food comes, the stage direction in the script tells the actors:

THE BUNDYS HAVE THEIR NAPKINS TIED AROUND THEIR NECKS AND EAT WITH THEIR HANDS. THEY SNORT THE FOOD LIKE PEOPLE WHO HAVEN'T EATEN IN DAYS.

THEY MAKE GRUNTING SOUNDS À LA THE CAVEMEN IN THE FILM *QUEST FOR FIRE*.

After they devour dinner in this boorish manner, Al says with great anticipation:

AL: There's only one way to top a meal like this…

Al summons the waiter for a newspaper, and as he tucks it under his arm and walks to the back of the restaurant, the studio audience knows exactly where Al is going and they howl because now instead of his usual verbal jokes scorning the upper class, he's literally taking a crap in the middle of one of their sacred spaces, a fancy restaurant.

However, when a blissful Al returns to settle up the bill and leave, he realizes he left his wallet home and quickly sends Bud and Kelly back to retrieve it. When the kids get home, however, they decide instead to filch the money to go to a rock concert and leave Mom and Dad in the lurch.

Back at their table, Peggy and Al realize their kids have abandoned them and they have no way to pay. As the waiters start to close in on them, the Bundys get an idea—Al takes off his shoes and flipping the script on his worst quality, foot odor, brandishes his shoes and socks as lethal weapons in the face of the oncoming staff who are so overcome by the stench that they clear a wide path for the Bundys to exit, which they do without paying their bill.

Barry Diller complained about crude bits like Al taking off his shoes to Fran McConnell, Embassy Studio senior vice president. Fran, a friend of Ron and his wife, Sharon, told Diller, "You're an East Coast sophisticate and most of the audience isn't. And there are more people out there like the Bundys than like the Keatons or the Huxtables. And these two writers (Ron and Michael) can deliver that because they're writing about their homes."

Gerry Cohen, also a close friend of Ron Leavitt's, said that the "Eatin' Out" episode was exactly like: "Going to a fancy restaurant with Ron. One of the first nights we were in London (shooting a *Married* vacation episode) we went to a nice restaurant. Ronnie got a steak. He sawed the chunk of meat, put it into his mouth and then he spat the piece of meat across the room with a joyful *coughing noise*."

Actor, Ted McGinley, who would later join the cast as Jefferson D'Arcy, also recalls dining with Ron at a fancy restaurant. "They give us a nice seat and next thing you know he orders like eight or nine coconut shrimp dishes for the table…and there's only six of us. And he orders one thing after the other and pretty soon they start throwing it. At first they're throwing a piece of buttered bread at each other and pretty soon we have a food fight in the middle of this fancy restaurant. He was like nobody else I'd ever met." Except, perhaps, Al Bundy.

Another episode that stretched the boundaries of the show and is also grounded in Al's obsession with his bowels was Katey Sagal's favorite, "A Dump of My Own." Here Al disrupts the entire household with a remodeling project that enables him to follow his childhood dream to please his father, which on any other sitcom, would trigger a touching, flashback tribute to dear old Dad, but on *Married… With Children.*

> **AL:** See, when I was a young boy I told myself when I grew up I would have one thing. (BEAT) A toilet bowl like my dad had. (PULLS A NEW, PLAIN WHITE

TOILET INTO THE ROOM) Not just a toilet. A Ferguson, the King of Bowls.

This sets up a classic moment later on when Al enters, ignoring Peggy completely, crosses to the Ferguson, gives the gleaming white toilet bowl a big hug, and says,

AL: Daddy loves you.

PEGGY: (MIFFED, TO MARCY) What does that toilet have that I don't?

AL: A job.

A great vehicle to highlight all of Christina Applegate's many talents in Season 3 was "Can't Dance, Don't Ask Me," where Kelly's punishment for teasing the school "Tap Club" was to perform a geeky tap dance at one of their upcoming concerts. Humiliated by this idea, Kelly instead breaks into a seductive dance in tandem with the hulky young school janitor, Bruno. This at first shocks the parents in the audience but soon they can't help but fall under the erotic spell of Kelly's gyrations and the grownups end up coupled off on the floor, making out with each other. Christina skillfully held the center of a demanding episode and displayed the dance skills that would years later award her a Tony nomination for her lead role in *Sweet Charity*.

We also pushed David into the spotlight, especially in "The Dateless Amigo," which played on David's lack of luck with girls and managed to turn the surreal nature of Kelly's teasing into a demanding routine of physical comedy for Bud.

KELLY: Bud, look at yourself, face the ugly truth. They don't have woods deep enough to grow the kind of girls that would be willing to date you. I mean, maybe you're aiming too high. You know, a live girl. See, your problem is you've got caviar taste and a pizza face. Aim a little lower. Hey, logs can't run away! And then there's the dead. You know, a girl who's been dead long enough might even think that you're a good catch. Hey, I know, how about a nice department store mannequin?

Though Bud is offended, he takes Kelly literally and tries to pass a department store mannequin off as his real date at a party with a few of his friends. Having pulled it off for most of the night, Bud, for the final move, starts carrying "Monique" upstairs to his bedroom until her limbs and other body parts start falling out one by one. Bud manages to resituate her limbs so that no one notices until later when Monique's head falls off her neck while he's dancing with her, which he barely but deftly conceals by "dipping" the rest of her body to the floor while surreptitiously reattaching her detached skull. David said that the whole bit never really came together in rehearsal but, inspired by the tension and vibe of a live audience, worked perfectly during the taping of the show and was what he loved about the multicamera form.

As Season 3 wound down, the ratings surge that followed Rakolta's protest earlier in the year kept building and was encouraging. Rakolta also became fair game in the *popular culture* she was attacking. "They made it a little personal when they wrote me into the scripts," Terry noted. In the *Married... With Children* episode, "Rock and Roll Girl," a TV announcer proclaimed that the band Gutter Cats were auditioning girls for the role of Rock Slut and that "*Eager young women came from as far as Bloomfield Hills, Michigan, to give it their all for the Gutter Cats.*" Bloomfield Hills is the suburb where Terry Rakolta lived.

A more direct hit came in episode when Marcy commented that FOX was cancelling one of their sitcoms because,

> **MARCY:** Some woman in Michigan didn't like it. She also didn't like football, so that's gone too.

The Simpsons also satirized Rakolta in the episode "Itchy, Scratchy and Marge," where Marge believes a particularly violent episode of the show-within-the-show influenced baby Maggie to knock Homer out with a mallet. In an obvious shot at Rakolta, Marge shoots off a nasty letter to the show's producers, forms a protest group to boycott the show, and appears on a talk show called *Smartline.*

Rakolta was undaunted and today still has no regrets. "Everybody won," she said. "I won because I was a warrior for value. At least for children. FOX won; they got more viewers than ever to their fledgling TV show. In a very small way I feel redeemed," she told me, especially proud because in some recent articles the press referred to her as "The Mother of Woke."

Rakolta went on to a successful career with her watch-dog group, Americans for Responsible Television, and later, as an advocate for the arts. *Married... With Children* went on to become one of the biggest hits in television history. Still, the question critic Ernie Smith posed in a recent article, remains: "The greatest *what-if* in television history might be this: What if Terry Rakolta had never been offended by *Married... With*

Children? Would we still have FOX? What would our moral standards for broadcast television be? I'm not sure, but I will say this: There's nothing like a moral panic to sharpen our popular culture." You're welcome.

POSTSCRIPT—CATCHPHRASES, CHARACTER QUIRKS, AND RUNNING GAGS

Sitcoms have been using catchphrases since Ricky told Lucy: "You've got some 'splainin' to do." Or Fred Flintstone exclaimed, "Yabba dabba do," or Vinnie Barbarino snapped, "Up your nose with a rubber hose." These "runners" as they are called, are guaranteed to get a quick laugh, however, their repeated use can also be a lazy way of forcing a chuckle, like J. J. Walker's incessant "Dy-no-mite!" which ultimately had little more resonance than flashing the laugh sign in front of the studio audience. *Married*'s catchphrases, though unapologetically designed to get quick laughs, were also used to satirize traditional sitcoms.

For example, Peggy's sardonic call for Bud and Kelly to, "Thank your father," was a shot at the cloying *Father Knows Best* messages still embodied in *The Cosby Show*, *Family Ties*, and *Growing Pains*.

> **PEGGY:** Kids, I think it's time we thank your father for bringing home minimum wage.
>
> **BUD/KELLY:** Thanks, Dad.

Or, as in Season 4's "It's a Bundyful Life, Part 2," when Peggy says:

PEGGY: Thank your father for flushing another Christmas, kids.

KELLY/BUD: (BITTERLY) Thanks, Dad.

Al calling Marcy, a chicken is an intentionally childish and reductive version of the more emotional and political clashes that regularly occur over Al's chauvinism and Marcy's feminism and are as closely associated with the show as Al sliding his hand down the front of his pants. The references started as early as Season 1's "Johnny B. Gone" when Marcy spilled a plate of fish on the floor and asked:

MARCY: Do you see a fish eye?

AL: (RE: MARCY'S BONY LEG) No, but I see a chicken leg.

We used it again in when Steve scolds the Bundys for lying on the kids' health forms:

STEVE: Uh, excuse me, but doesn't anybody know that this is against the law?

AL: So's dressing up a chicken and calling it your wife.

What really sold the bit, however, was an episode where Marcy turns to Steve, puts her hands on her hips and delivers her speech, bobbing up and down in a manner so closely miming a chicken she might as well be clucking the line:

MARCY: Why does he keep calling me a chicken?

The audience went wild and soon Al was making the chicken analogy on a regular basis. As when Marcy shows up at the front door holding a platter with a raw chicken on it.

AL: Marcy, I didn't know you were expecting.

Marcy, not to be outdone, equated Al with a variety of animals.

MARCY: You should be on all fours, carting a wagon full of borax across the desert. You're compost, you're phlegm, you are a true pork product!

Another popular runner was the Bundy family credo, satirizing platitudes spouted on other family sitcoms. The key one being: "A Bundy never wins, but a Bundy never quits." And:

AL: When one of us is embarrassed, the rest of us feel better about ourselves.

AL: Son, always remember the Bundy credo: lie when your wife is waking, lie when your belly's aching, lie when you know she's faking. Lie, sell shoes, and lie.

Other popular credos include:

- We don't eat vegetables.
- A Bundy never cares.
- We don't call the cops; they call the cops on us.
- When a Bundy doesn't get what's rightfully his, he makes sure that no one gets it either.

Then there's the Bundy cheer, aka, "Whoa, Bundy" celebrating family victories, like winning a fight.

AL: Kids, come over here, it's time for the Bundy cheer.

BUNDY FAMILY: Whoa, Bundy!

Variations include: "Whoa, Aliens!" "Whoa, cable!" and, "Whoa, stealing old ladies' pensions!"

Peg's main runner is her hatred of cooking and housework. Al jabs her about it when she says she wants a vacation

AL: Peg, if you wanna visit someplace new, try the kitchen. Oh, and why don't you get a picture of yourself with the refrigerator. You know, "Ol' Empty"?

Al also digs on Peggy's domestic proclivities as he gives some "fatherly" advice to the kids before taking them out to eat at a restaurant.

AL: Now kids, when we get to the restaurant something strange will happen. A woman will bring you food. Don't be scared, she's called a waitress. It's just God's alternative to Mommy.

These words, like most, are wasted on Kelly and Peggy:

KELLY: You know, Mom, when I grow up I want to be just like you. I want to do nothing. I want to be nothing.

PEGGY: (HUGGING KELLY) You make me so proud. I wish your father could hear that.

Another notable running bit is Al's extreme aversion to all things French. It starts briefly in Season 1 but by Season 5 it emerges in full glory when Al is desperately asking a French bakery owner about the whereabouts of his missing chef, Hans, who makes Al's favorite cheesecake.

> **AL:** (INTO PHONE) Listen, you French moron! We saved your cowardly wine-soaked behinds in the war! In all the wars! Every stinkin' war you've ever been in. Now you tell me where you're hiding Hans, before I… Hello!?! (AL HANGS UP, THEN) They really are rude to Americans!

This *cowardly* metaphor becomes one of Al's favorite ways to describe the French:

> **AL:**…running like a Frenchman from a cap gun.

> **AL:**…shaking like a Frenchman in a thunderstorm

The "Bundy Curse," is used extensively to explain and reconcile Bundy failures.

> **AL:** That's what keeps us from being happy. There's no point in fighting it. It's what separates us from the ordinary losers. They can have their moments. But not us. Never us…The minute a Bundy has good luck he immediately starts building up an equal amount of bad luck.

Al also held a grudge against the Kennedy family, which reflects his identification with the working guy and his bitter disdain of social class, fame, and political power. For example, when Bud tells Al he's uneasy about lying:

AL: Don't ever say that, son. The Bundys' proud name was built on a philosophy of lying. Well, lying, owing money, and perhaps beer. Yes, lying, owing money, and beer. The only thing that separates us from the Kennedys is that they have money.

The Kennedy name even made it into a verse of Al's "Nudie Bar" song:

AL: At the nudie bar, where the cops are at the door and there's a Kennedy on the floor.

Al's, often menacing *call to action*, "Let's rock," is another fan favorite, but the ultimate Bundy runner was Al's stinky feet. Originally, this was just an extension of his indifference to hygiene, like not bathing or brushing his teeth. As the series became increasingly broader and the response to his foot odor more *appreciated* by the audience, however, his malodorous feet became actual story devices, as in "Eatin' Out" where he actually weaponized his shoes or in "Married…With Aliens" where his foot stench was harvested by aliens to fuel their spaceship. But Al's stinky feet got the biggest laugh in a purely visual joke in "The Gypsy Cried," when Al takes off his shoes in the first-class section of an airplane, triggering the emergency oxygen masks to drop down from their hoses.

While some of our runners were satirical, they also functioned, Moye, said, "To establish the family as a team, needing no outside help. We hoped our audience could latch onto and thereby feel more included in the Bundy family dynamic."

Al and Peg shamelessly broke the rules of how couples behave in traditional family comedies.

It wasn't always pretty, but it was always funny and real.

In the end, you never doubted Al and Peg shared as deep a love as any couple on TV.

Christina was only 15 when she started playing Kelly so we saw all her *firsts* on TV.

First bleach job.

First bare midriff.

First garage band.

First waitress job.

First model job.

First whack job boyfriend that Al beat the crap out of.

Al's fantasy.

Al's reality.

David played the *lovable loser* who only dated blow-up dolls and mannequins with such deep commitment, fans loved him for it.

And on rare occasions, a real girl did too.

Al was known to drop a few hard-earned bucks on strippers at the Nudie Bar.

But when the tables were turned, he wasn't shy about trotting out his own *Big 'Uns.*

David Garrison and Ted McGinley opened the series up in totally different ways.

Steve brought out the cynical gadfly in Al.   Jefferson was more his comrade-in-arms.

Steve brought out the yuppie in Marcy.   Jefferson brought out the kinky.

These are the characters that revolutionized traditional family comedy on network television.

And these are the "characters" who created those characters:
Michael Moye and Ron Leavitt. *(Photo courtesy of Matt Leavitt)*

CHAPTER 10

SEASON 4: AL BUNDY VS. THE WORLD

HAVING SUCCESSFULLY FOUGHT OFF A near-fatal sponsor boycott in Season 3 (1988–1989) and emerging with a ratings spike that made *Married... With Children* the highest ranking show on FOX by the end of the season, one would have thought it would have been smooth sailing going into Season 4. One would have been wrong. Before the season even started, David Garrison announced he was leaving the series, and we were very concerned that losing a key member of our original foursome would seriously affect the chemistry and character balance of our show. The on-screen loss was magnified on a personal level, behind the scenes, because David was such a great guy to work with.

One of the most powerful tools a writer has to show the audience who a character really is is to show them who he or she really *isn't*. "We knew we had to have a counter to Al," Michael Moye pointed out, "and in order to drive Al nuts, Steve and Marcy would have to represent most of the things Al hated in life." Thanks to David Garrison's portrayal of Steve, we not only had a funny character in his own right, but a vehicle to define Al and get our audience to root for him.

MARCY: Just a second, Steve. I'm settling an argument here. Al is a cheap, sexist, primitive throwback of a human being.

STEVE: So, what's the argument?

The same holds for Steve helping to define Marcy, as when he gets revved up about muscle cars.

MARCY: Steve, where did you learn to talk like that?

STEVE: Hey, come on, honey, after all, I was a guy before I met you.

When Ed O'Neill heard that David Garrison wanted to leave the show, he took him to lunch to try to talk him into staying. David said that he enjoyed working on *Married... With Children* but he was leaving to return to his theatre career in New York. Ed also said that David told him that Ron and Michael had originally sold him on the idea that the show was like *The Honeymooners* and he was going to be Norton to Gleason's Kramden and now he was concerned that the "emergence of David and Christina would put him in the back seat." "There were only four people in *The Honeymooners* and no pet," Ed reminded him. "So, you couldn't have thought it was going to go exactly like that. *Married... With Children* had to feature everybody."

David understood all of that but his bottom line was, "I was basically commuting from New York to shoot the show in Los Angeles, and I missed my life in Manhattan as well as my theatre career. The first rule of show business is 'leave them wanting more,' After four seasons I felt it was time to exercise some other muscles." So, off he went to New York where he has had a stellar Broadway career in addition to several triumphant returns to *Married... With Children* as a guest star and some very notable roles in other TV series.

Besides losing a pivotal character and a fan favorite, David Garrison's take on portraying over-the-top, satirical characters such as ours was a role model for us all. "When you play parody," he believed, "you have to approach it as if it were the most serious thing in the world. You have to be deadly earnest, and it's in the deadly earnestness that the fun comes and the funny happens."

As sad as it was to see David go and as hard as it would be to make his departure believable, there were several factors that helped mitigate the damage. First of all, David's leaving was his own choice. There were no behind-the-scenes, backbiting scenarios that could easily have affected morale and performance. Ron and Michael loved David and his work, and would never stand in his way. They even gave him a parting gift to forever remember the show by—a poster of David's face with the caption underneath: "Gotta sing, gotta dance, gotta fucking starve to death."

Another factor working for us was that David had agreed to stay with the show for the first half of the upcoming fourth season. This gave us the opportunity to create a story arc for Steve that would make his exit from the series feel motivated, even inevitable. As you might expect, unlike other shows that strove to leave their audience with warm, fuzzy feelings about their departing characters, like on *Parks and Recreation* where Chris and Ann left to raise their new baby, *Married*'s goodbye kiss to Steve was to totally destroy his marriage and career at the same time.

Though it wasn't novel for Steve and Marcy to fight, it was almost always stoked by the spiteful Bundys, making it easier for them to reconcile and reset the series premise. This season, however, with David's departure in mind, we started to have Steve and Marcy's fights be totally self-motivated, causing friction that could not be mitigated by the realization that they had been duped by Peggy and Al. For example, in the first episode of Steve's last season, "Hot Off the Grill," Marcy enters the Bundy house carrying the ashes of her recently cremated aunt, all the while calling Steve, who enters with her, an "unfeeling cur" for disparaging her feelings about it.

> **STEVE:** Marcy, she's dead. Gone, fried, dust. Paying sailors in hell.
>
> **MARCY:** You know, Aunt Tuney never liked you.
>
> **STEVE:** She didn't like anything that didn't rub it's face back and forth across her potbelly.
>
> **MARCY:** Then, why didn't she like you?

Marcy and Steve keep bickering as the episode progresses. Then, Marcy gets her comeuppance when the entire group ends up inadvertently eating her "sainted" aunt's remains when her ashes are accidentally comingled with the burgers that Al is cooking on the barbeque.

In another ploy to *realistically* motivate Steve's move, we wrote him as increasingly frustrated with his job as a banker and the meaningless pursuit of money. He longed instead to devote himself to the joys of nature—an aspiration antithetical to the very basis of the Rhoadeses' bond as an upwardly mobile, Reagan-era, two Mercedes–owning couple.

Though we planted seeds along the way, the ultimate destruction of Steve's job and marriage came in one perfect storm, in the eighth episode, "976-Shoe." Steve, desperate to earn a bonus trip to Hawaii for giving the most loans from his bank, grants Al a $50,000 business loan for his crackpot idea of a launching a "976 Shoe-Hotline." The scheme, of course, implodes causing Steve to lose his job at the bank and Marcy to be demoted from loan officer to drive-in teller.

From here it was not much of a stretch to have Steve seek greater purpose by leaving Marcy to become a forest ranger. The final nail in the coffin of the Rhoadeses' marriage was Steve's goodbye letter to Marcy: "Frankly, I'm sick of you. You disgust me. I had a full head of hair when I met you, and I'm sure my nose grew during our marriage."

Although the series was losing a major character, viewers could see it as a successful outcome of Al and Peggy's goal from day one—to destroy Steve and Marcy's marriage and rub their faces in their shallow, yuppie ambitions. And, poetically, Steve's greedy and uncharacteristically ill-advised decision to use his position at the bank to try to help finance Al's crazy brainstorm was the final blow, or as Kelly put it in one of the first multiple malaprops she would become famous for:

KELLY: The squaw that stroked the camel's sack.

In upcoming plots, we then faced the challenge of who would occupy the physical and emotional space left by Steve's absence. The immediate solution was to keep pushing Bud and Kelly to the center and give them more significant roles in the stories. More pronounced Bundy teen drama would fill the vacuum with greater internal family conflict and comedically exploit the parentally challenged Bundys' limitations in problem-solving or dispensing advice, as when a lovelorn Bud reaches out to his father and asks:

> **BUD:** Dad, when you were in school, did a girl ever do something so horrible to you that it ruined your entire life?
>
> **AL:** Yes, and you call that girl "Mom" now.

Or in another Season 4 episode, when Kelly needs to ask her mom a question but she isn't around at the moment and Al tells her,

> **AL:** Listen, there's nothing that you can ask your mother that you can't ask me. Go ahead, shoot.
>
> **KELLY:** Okay. Well, I'm ovulating and when this happens I get this pinching little cramp. What should I do?
>
> **AL:** Walk it off. And remember, next time, stretch before you ov-a-late. (THEN) Bud?

Ed O'Neill recalls a particularly harsh father-son moment from this era—"I remember one time I was sitting on the couch and then David [Bud] sat next to me. He had a problem of some kind, and I was lamenting the fact that my Dodge looked like it was through. I said, you know, 'That car meant more to me than anything in my life,' and Bud said, 'W-w-what about me, Dad?' And I said—[yelled] 'Do you need a Q-tip?!' Most people would hear that and say, 'That's a terrible father," Ed continued, 'that's a dysfunctional family.' Well, guess what, they all are."

Another strategy in filling Steve's void was to expand Al's rage from antagonism of one particular yuppie who lived next door to an entire unfair system and a host of targets he perceived as holding the little guy down. We were essentially unleashing Al on the world. From the moment Steve left, for better or worse (and often both), Al took a bolo punch at everything in his reach—his boss, the beer tax, the aerobics craze, new car dealerships, do-it-yourself projects, the funeral industry, Jerry Springer, Kelly's boyfriends, Peggy's parents, Major League Baseball, the DMV, satellite TV, televangelism, and FOX sitcoms.

Consequently, the show morphed even further into a live action cartoon. "At this point," Moye admitted, "we were letting the audience drive. Meaning, we catered more and more to what our audience seemed to enjoy, and we sometimes sacrificed cohesion just to get the laugh." As Ed charitably put it: "After a while, you realize there are only so many shows you can do on the couch."

In Season 4, Peggy too, engages in class warfare, mocking cultural trends of the upwardly mobile. For example, in "Dead Men Don't Do Aerobics," Peggy gets a personal trainer, Jim Jupiter, who bills himself on his TV show as "The Healthiest Man in Chicago." She undermines his attempts to get her in shape, corrupting him with her cigarette smoking, junk food eating, couch potato lifestyle, precipitating a heart attack where he dies "live" on his own TV show. Perhaps Jim should have listened to Peggy when she said:

> **PEGGY:** Let's clear up a few misconceptions. There are two things Peggy Bundy doesn't do. Number one: cook, clean, sew, vacuum, iron, and parent. And number two: exercise.

Meanwhile, over on *The Cosby Show*, Clair hires a fitness trainer to shrink her into an old dress for an evening out with Cliff and *no one* dies.

Season 4 also produced another standout episode in the Al Bundy versus the world vein, "Who'll Stop the Rain." In this story, Peggy wants to call a roofer to fix their leaky roof, but Al takes a stand against Americans getting soft and lazy by deciding to fix it himself. Al's can-do spirit, however, is painfully blunted in repeated sequences of him falling off the roof, landing head-first on the patio. Al falling off the roof was so popular with our audience and became such a regular feature in subsequent episodes, we had a dummy made with Al's features to make it look more realistic and consequently, more hysterically painful.

Buck, the Bundy's dog, had always been a welcome sight in the Bundy living room, and he was occasionally used for a quick physical joke, as in the main titles where Buck reaches in to snag his share of the money Al is doling out to his greedy family. Or when Al complained that Peg never cooked for him while she secretly shoved a plate of food under the table for Buck to scarf down. The end of Season 4, however, marked the first time we actually heard Buck *speak* in an episode. Initially, this amounted to our audience *hearing* Buck's inner thoughts aloud, as in Season 4's, "Peggy Cooked a Little Lamb" when Peggy asks no one in particular what channel "Wheel of Fortune" is on and we are surprised to hear Buck's commentary.

BUCK: Uhh, it's seven, just like yesterday and the day before.

The audience response to this wry joke, voiced by writer Kevin Curran, combined with the amazingly appropriate *human* look on Buck's face, finessed by his trainer Steven Ritt, was so strong that it inspired us to expand Buck's character for the rest of the series. Buck ended up with voiceover lines in fifty-seven subsequent episodes, and, in three of them, his character was the central plot device for the story. Not in any way a replacement for losing Steve, but a welcome tool for the series nonetheless.

However, the post–Steve era episode that has become one of the all-time fan favorites was a Season 4 two-parter where *Married* flies its satirical flag high in a spoof of the classic film, *It's a Wonderful Life*, aptly titled, "It's a Bundyful Life." The show featured Sam Kinison playing the angel who has come down from heaven to show a disconsolate Al what life on earth would have been like had he never been born. Ted McGinley, who would later be cast as Jefferson, played the man Peggy would have married if Al had never existed, the handsome, wealthy socialite, Norman Jablonsky. In this upside down take on the original film, Peggy is happy, Bud and Kelly possess uncharacteristic genius and social prowess, and consequently, the spiteful Al, looking in from the outside on all of this, decides to live and give his family another shot.

Sam Kinison's appearance on *Married* was the focus of considerable attention on the set. Although people were drawn to his eccentric charisma, his attention-getting antics on the stage made working with him a challenge and provided some eye-opening examples of what he would have been like to work with on a regular basis if he had accepted the original offer to play Al.

He started off on the wrong foot, or butt cheek as it were, mooning the cast from the wings during a rehearsal. Although he made amends to the actors by inviting them to his birthday dinner at Spago that night, the incident was not soon forgotten. Nor was it the last such occurrence.

Sam then showed up late for a rehearsal. "So the next day," Ted McGinley remembers, "to make it up for everybody he had lunch catered by Chasen's [a famous L.A. restaurant at the time] and he had it served to us by strippers. I hadn't even seen the show so I didn't know what I was getting into. I had only been on *Happy Days* and *Love Boat* and I said, this is like 'What?!' I had so much fun that week."

"Sam was crazy, but sweet," recalls Amanda Bearse. "And kinda sad, really."

"I loved him," Katey Sagal remembers. "I absolutely loved him. He was bigger than life, kindhearted, huge hearted, brought us presents. I saw him a couple of times socially out and he would always call me an angel. You know, I am a sober person, and I would see him out and about, and he was *not*. He would keep me by his side at all times."

Gerry Cohen, who had the task of directing the outrageous comic in the two-part episode, told me: "I was initially pretty skeptical about casting Sam, and the first couple days of rehearsal he was just sort of riffing around the material. It was a little chaotic at first because I was trying to force the square peg of Sam Kinison into the round hole of this script. But once Sam recognized the value of what was on the page for him, he really came around and by the time we shot that episode, it was like we had been friends for a very long time."

That friendship and every other friendship Sam fostered while on the show was put to a rather extreme test shortly thereafter. At the time, Gerry was dating a woman who would one day become his wife, who, as it happens, was also friends with Sam. Gerry recalls, "I woke up one night at about two in the morning and I went—'Oh, girlfriend's not home.' She was supposed to be home a while ago. And this was in the days immediately preceding the ubiquitous cell phone. I had a hunch and I got into my car and I drove to Sam's house and I knocked loudly on the front door, and the door cracked open and a .45 caliber automatic pistol came out through the crack of the door and Sam put it within an inch of my forehead. Then Sam looked at me and I looked at him and he said, 'Ger...what are you doing here?' I said, 'Sam, you know damn well what I'm doing here.' He said, 'Well, I could shoot you.' I said, 'Yeah, and we both know you're not going to,' and I pushed the door open and went in the house, got my girlfriend, and went home." With that, Gerry gave us an object lesson on why he was so well suited at directing the irascible comic and also why it was a fortunate for us that Sam had turned down the role of Al Bundy when it was offered to him.

In another bizarre twist to the story, Gerry and Sam remained friends for the rest of Sam's life, which was only three years later when Sam, having just returned from his honeymoon in Hawaii, was driving to a gig in Branson, Missouri, when a teenager driving a pickup truck hit him head-on, causing injuries from which he died shortly thereafter.

While we're on the subject of guns, dating, and *Married... With Children* (a good title, by the way), when David Faustino was sixteen he went out on a date with an actress who played a love interest of his on the show, Stefanie Ridel. After he picked her up and was walking her to his car in Hollywood, however, two gangbangers pulled guns on them. David said, "It was pretty much an immediate gun-to-the-head situation…, like, 'give me your shit.' I kind of thought this was the end when one of the gunmen said: "Hey, you're Bud Bundy from *Married… With Children*, aren't you?" And they just kind of backed off into the darkness of the night and fled." Besides being grateful that Bud Bundy, in essence, saved his life, David noted that, "The show at the time was really in its heyday. And everyone was watching it, including criminals."

David went out with Stefanie for a little bit after that, but he was philosophical when they stopped seeing each other: "After a first date like that, how can it get any more exciting?"

"It's a Bundyful Life" turned out to be a classic *Married* episode, and further, it garnered the highest ratings ever for FOX (18.4, breaking into the week's top twenty network shows for the first time and beating such highly rated sitcoms as *Who's the Boss?* and *Coach*, which regularly ranked higher than us). Steve would be greatly missed and he would return for guest appearances several times, to the delight of the studio audience. However, there was no doubt that this was the end of an era for the show and no one was really sure what would happen next season, except, with the ratings bump, for the first time at the end of a season, we felt confident there would be another one.

POSTSCRIPT—*MARRIED*'S CRYSTAL BALL

When you're writing a television show like *Married… With Children*, there's no better feeling than walking into a bar or a restaurant or down the street and overhearing someone saying something that you wrote for a character, like "Let's rock," or "Whoa, Bundy." Or to be at a Halloween party or a dance club and see a woman (or a man) coiffed in a highly teased red wig, wearing Capri pants and mules, camping it up, walking with Peggy's signature sashay.

These character idiosyncrasies are well planned and their sightings are a concrete way of knowing your show is having an impact. However, when you're on the air for eleven years, which we would eventually be, you can't help but make jokes, bits, and references that were totally random at the time but when viewed in hindsight, have an eerie sense of clairvoyance. For example, in "God's Shoes," Al has the get-rich-quick idea to invent "toe shoes," essentially a glove for the foot. Al's idea is a bust, but five years later, that same product was put out by the Vibram company under the name Five Fingers and is still on the market.

Similarly, Al's "Shoelights," which he invented for walking in the dark, were a total disaster in one episode, practically electrocuting Kelly who was wearing them in a trial run. Over thirty years later, a for-real shoe light called Bright Feet came out, featuring small LED lights to shine the way, and they are also still on the market.

Peggy, a huge daytime TV talk-show fan, mentioned once in an episode that she was going to watch the show that directly followed Oprah, which we dubbed, *Oprah After the Show-prah*. Years later, Oprah added her own post-Oprah series, called *Oprah After the Show*, a remarkably close, though arguably less catchy title.

In our first season we learned that Al had been banned from attending Chicago Cubs' games at Wrigley Field and reviled by the entire city because he interfered with a ball that was in play, which resulted in keeping the Cubs out of the World Series. Uncannily, sixteen years later, Steve Bartman did almost exactly the same thing at Wrigley Field during the 2003 National League Championship Series, which also kept the Cubs out of the World Series. Bartman was heckled by fans and had his life threatened as he was escorted by police out of the stands.

In a two-parter when Kelly goes to Hollywood to become a children's television host, she makes a prima donna demand that they give her purple M&Ms only to be told they don't exist. Five years later the Mars Company would come out with purple M&Ms. Thirty years later, their commercials, which featured multicolored animated M&Ms dancing in stiletto heels and go-go boots were cancelled because they "perpetuate sexist stereotypes."

In another episode, Bud offers Kelly's bathwater for sale as a throwaway line, and now Instagram star Belle Delphine makes millions of dollars selling hers and no one seems to be protesting that she's perpetuating sexist stereotypes.

In 1987, Jerry Hall, Mick Jagger's ex-wife, was a guest star as a stewardess girlfriend of Al's coworker, Luke, in the episode "Al Loses His Cherry." Almost thirty years later, Rupert Murdoch married Jerry Hall and, though she gave a memorable performance on our show, I doubt our billionaire boss was influenced by or even saw her stellar work in *Married... With Children*.

In Season 5's "Kids! Wadaya Gonna Do?," Buck said to Bud (in Buck's voice-over),

BUCK: "And at least I have the decency to die at thirteen."

Five years later, Buck actually died at the age of thirteen.

Finally, many years after Al takes off his shoes while flying on an airliner and the unbearable odor causes the plane's oxygen masks to be activated and drop down, an American Airlines flight made an emergency landing after an odor described as "dirty sock smell" caused crew members to feel nauseous. Recently, the Cabin Air Safety Act bill was introduced in Congress to protect passengers and crew from what has been deemed, "toxic cabin air." This came after a number incidents where airline passengers complained of burning throats and chest pains, said to have been caused from a "dirty socks" odor.

CHAPTER 11

SEASON 5: MARRIED...
WITHOUT STEVE

SEASON 5, BESIDES BEING THE midway year in the eleven-season *Married... With Children* run, also marked the tipping point of the creative divide between the satirical, more grounded trajectory of the first half of the series and the broader, more cartoonish flight of the second. Simultaneously, however, a different type of shift took place for those of us working on the show. The type of character conflict that was so refreshing and rewarding for us to create for our fictional family on the screen was now creeping into our work family, behind the scenes. In other words, life was starting to imitate art, or whatever you want to call what we do for a living.

Michael Moye was especially affected by this turn of events. "While the first half of the series was viewed as fun and the realization of an antisitcom dream, the second half put me in a place of bitterness, sarcasm and a mistrust of society that I carry to this day," he recalled. "I began to approach each day waiting for the other shoe to drop and many days I was not disappointed. I was constantly at odds with the business affairs department over what I perceived to be their frugality and lack of promotion. I was also at odds with the network over what I perceived to be their total misunderstanding of our antisitcom message, especially after the Rakolta Effect. My only solace became the writing room where I finally felt I was amongst like-minded people who had a grasp on what we were trying to do." Even there, Michael conceded, "I had to deal with everything from trying to counsel writers' love affairs to working through writers just not getting along. It really became a game of dodging bullets."

Though my fellow writers and I were aware of the added tensions during this period, it's a tribute to Michael's and Ron's leadership skills and all-around good nature that they didn't let the bigger issues that were pressing on them from the network and the studio trickle down to us and poison our demanding but otherwise high-spirited work atmosphere. As the years progressed, however, the problems became harder to deflect, the stakes much higher, and the obstacles more formidable to our job of putting on a weekly television show.

Besides the internal conflicts between the creatives and the executives that aggravated Moye so deeply, the stage turned out to be the breeding ground of some very intense personal battles between certain actors, which, as you will soon see, would rage out of control as the seasons progressed right down to the very end of the series, and, as I discovered in writing this book, to this day.

In hindsight, I think during the first few seasons, the normal workplace tensions that naturally emerge in an environment such as ours were channeled into what I would call a *mission mentality*—the unusual amount of energy expended and freedom granted to us in working as a team to fight the *good fight* for the very life or death of our underdog show. This mission mentality, with which we all identified, was enough reward for those of us in the trenches (and the command posts) to overlook the usual daily squabbles that arise in most business settings. Now, however, that our biggest struggles were *seemingly* behind us and not every fight was an existential one, the type of ego and personality conflicts that had been hitherto tamped down were unleashed and dramatically changed the tenor of the workplace in the later years of the series.

Regardless of what was going on behind the scenes, however, we were keenly aware of the task at hand of putting on a weekly show and even though we had cleared many unusual hurdles in the first four seasons, this fifth season (1990–1991) presented us with some creative challenges that required as much concentration and dedication as we had ever had.

Season 4 showed we could adapt to losing Steve by giving Bud and Kelly more screen time and broadening the targets of Al's vexations, but there was still a lot more to accomplish creatively as we headed into Season 5. Steve had still been in half of the episodes last season but would be totally gone this year, so we would have to double our efforts to fill that story gap and still deliver on the premise of the show that had gotten us to this point. FOX, as a network, was also starting to have success with some of its other shows, so we could no longer get by, as we had to some extent, by simply being the biggest star on the smallest network.

Season 5's opening episode, "We'll Follow the Sun," thus had a lot riding on its shoulders—filling the gap left by Steve, setting a broader tone for the series, and attracting new viewers while trying to hold on to our return customers. We wasted no time in doing that: in the very first shot of the episode, we see a portable radio on the Bundy kitchen table and hear a cheery DJ, hawking,

DJ: (V.O.) "Show me an unhappy man today and I'll show you a—"

Al finishes the thought as he smashes the radio to smithereens with a baseball bat—

AL: A shoe salesman, Jim. A 20th-century blacksmith. A workingman. An idiot.

Then Peggy enters and we see the marriage is as delightfully combative as it ever was…maybe more.

PEG: Hi honey. Did you miss me?

AL: With every bullet so far.

PEG: Well, maybe you need a bigger gun, sweetheart, not that I don't love your itty-bitty one.

Kelly enters, proudly waving her high school diploma. When she asks Peggy to read the diploma to her so she knows what it says, however, we are reassured that, even though she graduated, she will be as delightfully ditzy as ever. Bud enters, confident that his senior year will change his luck with the ladies until he learns from Kelly that even "the Malaysian mail-order bride company" rejected him.

Al then suggests a family road trip to cheer everyone up, and teases the audience with one of our new series goals: that the shoe man is about to take us beyond the scope of Steve, the Bundy couch, the store and, even the neighborhood.

AL: We're gonna see America. We'll stay in cheap motels and steal what we need along the way. Where the air is fresh, the sky is big, and a man can still kill his dinner with his car.

The rest of the show plays like an episode of *WWE SmackDown!* as the road-tripping Bundys get stuck in a massive holiday traffic jam that pits the family against each other until another stalled driver insults Al, causing the Bundys to unite, pull the offending driver and his family out of their car, and brutally pummel them to the ground. This sets up an opportunity for one of Al's everyman speeches, which he delivers like a storefront preacher from the altar of the hood of the Dodge.

AL: What about us, the ones who truly labor? We're on this stinking road every day, choking and wheezing, marching along like lemmings to a horrible, screaming death. Who cries for us, Argentina? The yoke on the oxen feels no guilt. But what we can expect is that on our one lousy stinkin' day off, traffic can move us to our lousy stinkin' pathetic destinations. To our polluted beaches, our burning forests, our wheezing grandmas. To our family barbeques with Uncle Otto and his runny eye. But does the highway department prepare for us? Are they out here helping us? Are they out there in front of us by that first damn car that caused this traffic jam, saying, "Step on the gas, you moron! Let the 20 million people pass!"? They are not. Why? Because they don't care. And that, my friends, is what really reeks!

Al's speech makes him a workingman's hero to the crowd and gets traffic moving until a moment later when Al gets a flat tire, which holds up traffic even more and causes him to be stormed by a tire iron–wielding mob...the same crowd that moments ago lionized him. The recurring Bundy family character themes plus the extension of Al's targets from the home, the neighborhood, and the shoe store out to the world, along with his victory turning to shit, makes it a perfect opening episode for the fifth season— welcoming new fans into the fold, introducing new themes into the show, while assuring die-hards we can still deliver the goods.

Unfortunately, the same can't be said about the seventh episode of the season, "Married...With Aliens." Though popular with many fans, this episode dives deeper into the cartoon swamp than the series has ever plunged, as little green aliens invade the Bundy home, desperate to collect the stench from Al's socks as fuel to power their spaceship home. Peggy, unlike Al, does not see the aliens, which, at least grounds the story in some version of reality and character humor:

> **PEGGY:** Al, you banged your head tonight. You are having a hallucination. You're probably seriously hurt and require immediate medical attention. Now go to sleep.

Then, at the end of the show, when all the photos Al took of the aliens (hoping to fetch millions from the tabloids) are accidentally ruined by the photo developer, Al is back where he started, broke and *Married... With Children*.

Critic Jason Upperco, while acknowledging the downside of season's drift into *unreality*, also points out the upsides of entering this era with the show: "The series enters its fifth year with a looseness regarding intention; no longer does it have to satirize or mock…now it's ready to play with the characters and soar to new comedic heights." This was especially true of a two-parter, "You Better Shop Around," which always ranks high in fans' favorite *Married* episodes. During an extreme heat wave, when the Bundys' power is blown out, they seek shelter in an air-conditioned supermarket where they stretch out on lounge chairs in front of the chilled beverage section and behave as if they're enjoying a fun day at the beach rather than simply being freeloading squatters in a grocery store. This sets up a spoof of a *Supermarket Sweep* game, Bundys versus D'Arcys, where a super competitive and spiteful Al runs his shopping cart so aggressively over a fallen Marcy that he leaves deep wheel tracks on her back.

The concept of using Buck's inner voice for quick laughs was expanded exponentially in Season 5 in an episode totally driven from the family dog's point of view. Feeling neglected by the Bundys, Buck decides to run away from home which, of course, no one notices. After an encounter on the city streets with an empathic B.B. King who sings him a blues song, Buck, in a "Lady and the Tramp" turn is smitten on a cute female dog behind a diner who he decides to impress by bringing her off the streets and into his home. Buck quickly regrets the decision, however, when the new dog gets all the attention Buck was longing for in the first place. This was the first of three episodes where Buck was voiced by Cheech Marin.

This season also saw *Married* satirizing one of the most sacred cows of domestic comedy, the sitcom wedding, which was such go-to area that *Friends* squeezed eight of them into its ten years on the air. *Married*'s take on the holy bonds thereof finds a very drunk Marcy stumbling into the Bundys', having just gotten married to someone but too drunk to remember exactly to whom she was sworn to *honor and obey till death do them part.* It turns out to be Jefferson D'Arcy (Ted McGinley, who played Norman Jablonsky in "It's a Bundyful Life), a dashing, shiftless gigolo who, once he moves in with Marcy, is played as a sidekick to Al rather than the stiff alter ego Steve had been.

Even as the show pushed into the fringe areas of little green aliens and supermarket sweeps, Michael and Ron always managed to find some small, personal stories that gave unexpected insight into the human condition, like Season 5's "The Dance Show." The action starts with a typical Al/Peggy squabble that drives Peggy to hang out with Marcy at a local bar, where an attractive man, Andy, takes a liking to Peggy and dances the night away with her. A smitten Peggy keeps going back to dance with Andy, all the while trying to warn her oblivious husband that it's becoming "harder and harder to fend off the men" at the club.

One night after Peggy leaves to go dancing with Andy at the bar, Pete (played by Dan Castellaneta, the voice of Homer Simpson), shows up at the Bundy house to tell Al that Peggy has been *seeing* his husband at the bar. After Al sorts out the fact that Pete and Andy are a gay couple, he gets to know Pete and grows fond of him, as he is more of his ideal of a real *wife* than Peggy.

> **AL:** Wait a minute. You work, you cook, and you like sports?
>
> **PETE:** Yeah, except for soccer. That's not really a man's game.
>
> **AL:** I love you.

Pete eventually convinces Al to talk Andy into coming back, as he fears Peggy will lure him back into the straight life. A sympathetic Al enters the bar and abruptly pulls Andy from Peggy, who still doesn't know he's gay.

> **AL** (TO ANDY): Look, I don't care what you're doing with my wife. But you got a good man at home that any man would be proud to call his wife. He cooks, he cleans, he works. You've obviously gotten over that little "he's a man" thing. So, what else do you want from the poor guy?

Al's convinces Andy to go back to Pete and inspires the lowly shoe man to tell Peggy how much he loves her. Al's defense of marriage, straight or gay, never gets too saccharine or self-congratulatory, but just when you fear that Al might be slipping into a *teaching moment*, he bluntly says to Peggy, who doesn't realize Andy is gay and is still boasting about how attracted he was to her:

> **AL:** He was a homo, Peg.

As anachronistic as that term is, the website TV Tropes, in an article about this episode, points out that, in general, *Married* was…"more progressive (than other sitcoms) for its day." The article goes on to cite another episode, "Dud Bowl," where Al's football teammates from high school reunite years later for another sitcom staple—"one more game"—and they discover one of their old buddies, Thad, is transgender—*not* a sitcom staple.

> **THAD:** I had to do it, Al. All those years I felt like a woman trapped inside a man's body.

We can tell by how Thad and Peggy greet each other that they regard Thad as the same person she was in high school. Furthermore, Thad is still eager to play in the football game and her old teammates are glad to have her. During the episode, no one treats Thad any differently, except one guy who treats her gender as a joke and she promptly punches him out.

According to another website, Bundyology, which also commented on this episode, "The closest thing to a transphobic joke is Al being squeamish about Thad's penectomy while also making it clear that he doesn't think Thad's identity as a woman should *demand* she transition medically, which is remarkably progressive even into the 2010s."

Season 5 also commemorated *Married... With Children*'s landmark one hundredth episode with a planted spin-off starring a pre-*Friends* Matt LaBlanc as Vinnie, a down-on-his-luck boxer who once had a fling with Kelly but his master plan, devised by his father (Joseph Bologna) is for the dim-witted, classless Vinnie to hook up with a rich, young society woman. The series, *Top of the Heap*, had a short run on FOX where it spawned another short lived spin-off, *Vinnie and Bobby*.

Another new series runner, which would turn out to be very controversial, was the introduction of Al's favorite TV show, *Psycho Dad*, a Western version of *Married*, as evidenced by its theme song.

> *Who's that riding into the sun?*
> *Who's the man with the itchy gun?*
> *Who's the man who kills for fun?*
> *Psycho Dad,*
> *Psycho Dad,*
> *Psycho Dad.*

By the end of the season, our questions about how our creative adjustments would play with our audience were answered when we garnered FOX network's highest rating of all time—number three for the week—and any threat to our longevity was dispelled. Leavitt and Moye, however, were always so much more tuned into the creative needs of the series than calculating the business needs that Michael was able to look back and honestly say, "FOX had nothing at all to do with these character and story decisions. By Season 5 with stories harder to come by, Ron and I made a conscious decision to take some of our cues directly from our audience. We observed that Al had become more than just a relatable character by now, he had become a spokesman for the everyman, a demographic very few sitcoms concerned themselves with. As far as the expansion of the Bud and Kelly roles, not only were they older, which made it easier to add more depth to their characters but, by then, they had really grown on the audience. So, again, we let the audience drive. We were just cool going along for ride."

It would have been impossible to predict, however, just how bumpy that ride would turn out to be in Season 6 when an unforeseen misfortune, having nothing to do with the ratings, the creative challenges of the year, or the internal personal conflicts that were brewing behind the scenes had an even more profound effect on the show and everyone working on it.

POSTSCRIPT—FOUR TOUCHDOWNS IN ONE GAME AND THE EXALTED PLACE OF SPORTS IN *MARRIED... WITH CHILDREN*

The spotlight on sports in *Married... With Children* appeared from the opening bell of the first episode when Al and Peggy had a sparring match over whether he could to go to the Chicago Bulls game instead of staying home to meet their new neighbors, Steve and Marcy (Peggy won in a knockout). The rest of the episode also played out like a sporting event with Al and Peggy teaming up in a rapid-fire verbal bout against the newlyweds, who were so outmatched by Team Bundy they threw up their arms and fled the house in defeat.

Married's grounding in sports themes, however, started long before that. Moye recalls, "My father was the kind of guy who worked in a factory. He drove a truck. He would come home. He would turn on the TV. All he cared about was baseball and pro wrestling. He didn't want to hear from the news. He didn't want to know any socioeconomic stuff. He just wanted to be entertained through sports, and, when he was sleepy, sitcoms."

Leavitt and Moye themselves were also huge sports fans and picked the name "Bundy" as an homage to pro wrestler King Kong Bundy, who later appeared in two episodes. Steve Rhoades was named after wrestling great Dusty Rhodes. Al honored his only son by naming him after one of the biggest name in sports, Bud Light.

Married did so many sports stories that FOX ran a special half-hour compilation show, hosted by TV sports commentator Roy Firestone called the *Al Bundy Sports Spectacular*. There were clips of everything from simple, internal domestic sports stories, which furthered the premise, like Peggy beating Al's all-time high bowling score, to elaborate, high-concept stories, starring some of the biggest names in the history of sport—Terry Bradshaw, Sugar Ray Leonard, Joe Namath, Johnny Bench—that not only saluted sports but underscored the very relatable fact that many guys like Al love to escape their current days as washed-up, married working stiffs by trying to relive their glory days as exalted athletes (whether they were or not).

But the heart and soul of *Married... With Children*'s sports stories and the crowning achievement in Al's life was the real story of him scoring four touchdowns in a one game in high school. "The idea of scoring four touchdowns in a single game came about," according to Moye, "because Ron and I didn't want to create a fellow who was cursed out of the womb. We thought the man would be much more relatable if the sun shone on him every once in a while, even if the last time was a long time ago. The one thing we were sure of was that it had to have happened before he was married and saddled with a family and that meant high school or college."

"We created an entire backstory that came out in one episode" Michael recalls, "about how he was recruited by college football scouts [which Ed O'Neill actually was by the Pittsburgh Steelers] until one night, while drunk, Peggy dared Al that he couldn't leap over a moving vehicle like some pro she'd seen on TV. Al tried and—

> **AL:** I was two inches short, Peg. If my toe had just cleared the driver's nose I would've won that ten dollars. *And* that fight with Jack. And played college ball. And married a debutante. And been rich and happy.

(LOOKS AT PEGGY) But, things worked out just great anyway. I have no complaints. Oh, God.

The first time Al actually mentioned his epic "four touchdowns in one game" saga at length was in telling Kelly a bedtime story when she was having trouble falling asleep.

> **AL:** Once upon a time there was a man who sold shoes. He was a good man but somehow good things never came to him. Did I mention he was a great athlete in high school? People cheered him. That was before the… Red Thing appeared. Darkness fell on Shoe Town. Who would take on the Red Beast? Who would battle? Who would marry her? The little shoe man stepped forward. Or perhaps the others just stepped back. At any rate, an unholy union was born. So were two unholy children. And the lowly shoe man, who had once been a mighty athlete in high school and scored four touchdowns in one game and had many offers to junior college and could have made something of his life…laid down… and died. The end.

Al's "four touchdowns in one game" became such a hallmark of the series and so deeply ingrained in the lowly shoe salesman's character that the legend is still very much alive in the culture today. It got a lot of play from network TV commentators, recently when Travis Kelce of the Super Bowl champion Kansas City Chiefs scored four touchdowns in a game against the Las Vegas Raiders. Afterwards, Ed sent Travis an Instagram that went viral, congratulating him on tying Al Bundy's all-time record. Travis tweeted back that, "Al Bundy has been my role model my entire life," then posted a picture of Al from the show, referring to himself as the "Modern Day Al Bundy."

Gerry Cohen told me he watched the broadcast of Kelce's record-breaking game and when one of the anchors jokingly dismissed Travis's feat, because—"Al Bundy scored four touchdowns in one game," years ago, he was sorry that "Ron Leavitt [who died years before] didn't get to experience that moment of how we are still part of the culture today."

had. David Garrison, returning for a guest spot, recalls how, most overnight, "From a Friday when we wrapped the show to onday when we came in to read the next one, Christina went m being an adorable, talented teenager to the gorgeous young man who would break out as a comedy star in all fields."

Kicking off Kelly's new character direction was "Kelly Does llywood." In Part 1, Kelly gets her own talk show on cable ', *Vital Social Issues N' Stuff With Kelly*, where she dishes with girlfriends on hot topics like "men's butts" and "the slut of week," mocking cable talk shows and the ever emerging troll- side of social media. Kelly's local TV show becomes so pop- r it is picked up by a "real" network, NBS, a not-so-subtle t at NBC.

In Part 2, when Kelly shows up in Hollywood for a meet- at NBS headquarters, *Married* takes the opportunity to e shots at traditional networks as we see posters promoting BS's lineup—*Ellen and Her Dog*, *Black Cop, White Girl, Me d the Shiksa*, and *The Homeless Detective*. The satire becomes n more pointed when NBS changes everything they originally ed about Kelly's talk show, which leads to it being cancelled.

Though Kelly's Hollywood dreams are crushed by the con- sion of this episode, Christina's portrayal of a ditzy wannabe ress was so funny and crowd pleasing it gave rise to more Kelly wbiz-themed roles. Most famously, as The Verminator—a erhero commercial spokesperson for the environmentally sponsible Pest Boys Extermination Co.

Just as Kelly's portrayal of an aspiring young actress became ular in our show, Christina landed her first film role in *Don't Mom the Babysitter's Dead* which led her to more films,

CHAPTER 12

SEASON 6: MARRIED... WITH MORE CHILDREN

SEASON PREMIERE EPISODES, BESIDES BEING tools to fire up the fan base, are often used to billboard exciting new series mile- stones and bring more people than ever to the party, which is why FOX felt it had a goldmine on its hands with the opening of Season 6 (1991–1992).

TV ANNOUNCER: Brace yourself for the ultimate on FOX: Al Bundy is expecting his third child!

Al, as you might expect, had a slightly different take.

AL: I feel like Exxon. One spill and I'm paying for it for the rest of my life.

Backing up a little, in real life, Katey Sagal had become preg- nant before Season 6 began. What that generally means to an ongoing production is that the actress is shot with camera angles to hide her baby bump, and the writers have to contrive a reason as to why she is "missing" for whatever time it takes the actress to give birth and return. However, in this case, "My supermenschy bosses, Ron Leavitt and Michael Moye," Katey said, "decided it made perfect sense that Peggy Bundy might get pregnant and asked if I would be okay with them writing my pregnancy into the show. I thought that was a fantastic idea. I found Ron and Michael to be such big-hearted guys, even under those dirty T-shirts with pizza stains on them."

"Ron and I," Michael said of their decision to accommodate Katey's pregnancy, "never forgot these *characters* of ours were real people as opposed to just tools we used to do a job for us until the next show came around. So, whenever a personal issue came along, we tried to prioritize it because *they* needed to prioritize it."

As it happened, from a writing standpoint, having a new *Bundy* baby also worked to enhance the original premise of the series and further burden Al and the kids.

PEGGY: Now kids, I don't want you to be jealous of the baby, I'll always have time for you. After all (she strokes Bud's face) you were my first.

KELLY: Uh, I was your first.

PEGGY: Really? Oh well, what's important now is the baby.

Adding a child to a show was hardly an historical event. Little Ricky joined *I Love Lucy* as far back as 1953. History also teaches us that adding a child to a series doesn't always work as *The Brady Bunch* was cancelled five episodes after adding Cousin Oliver.

When FOX promoted a Bundy baby for Season 6, however, our premiere (which also featured Marcy being pregnant) hit an historical FOX ratings high—number two for the night, drawing 29.2 million viewers, making it the highest-ranked series in the six-year history of the FOX Network. Whatever pride we

took from those opening numbers, though, was by Episode 6, when Katey's pregnancy tragically stillborn child.

After this happened, Michael Moye wanted it (in the storyline of the series) in the least maud not put too much of an emotional burden on ou our own people. So we did what *Dallas* did and m season a dream but even more cartoony."

Katey said it was a "perfect solution" but sh make peace with her unfathomable loss and it di the tabloids were: "Lurking. Looking for dirt. H unflattering pic. For deeper insight my answer cam teachings. Ruby's purpose had been fulfilled in the was here. She gave me greater appreciation for life i to mention the whole childbirth thing. What a fu that is." Now, happily, Katey has two daughters an

As heartbreaking as it was to chart a new course in the middle of Katey's tragedy, the timeworn clic must go on—rang true. With Katey's boundless co professionalism and hard work of the entire staff, c writers during the remainder of Season 6, we pr memorable shows and significant character develop turned out to be as much a part of the *Married* other season and, happily, also tapped deeper into th personal ambitions and desires as never before.

For example, Kelly Bundy's aspiration to be a n commercial spokesperson, and so forth turned out t fit for Christina Applegate who fiercely inhabited if everything in her life had been building to this

including the *Anchorman* series with Will Ferrell. She also won an Emmy for her role as Rachel's sister on *Friends* and starred in several other TV series, including the highly acclaimed *Dead to Me*.

Season 6 was also a breakout year for David Faustino. The writers stole a page out of David's real-life aspirations in a new medium that was blowing up at the time, hip-hop. David not only recorded a rap album, *Balistyx*, he also cofounded the first hip-hop funk club on the Sunset Strip (also called, Balistyx). Balistyx was a huge hit, featuring such major artists as Eazy-E and will.i.am. "I wouldn't have had my record deal with Eazy-E," said, willi.i.am, of the Black Eyed Peas, "if it hadn't been for David Faustino." Balistyx was also a hang for such future stars as Leonardo DiCaprio, Tobey Maguire, and Fergie. David is still active in the hip-hop scene.

"The writers knew how much of a hip-hop head I was," David recalls. "I would bring hip-hop cats around and they were like, 'What's this kid doing?' They didn't really understand it but they found a way to poke fun at it," and, even more importantly, to poke fun at Bud. Early in Season 6, Bud announced that hip-hop was going to be his way to bury his past and finally get laid.

> **BUD:** As of now my story is that I'm a bad boy rapper from the streets of New York. Goodbye Bud Bundy, hello Grandmaster B.

Bud began to have sporadic success with girls in the series, but whenever he got cocky about his new Grandmaster B image, he could count on his family to put him back in his "lovable loser" place.

> **KELLY:** Oh, forgive me, Ghostbuster B.

Or after Peggy addresses him as Grand Marshal B, which prompts Kelly to *correct* her.

KELLY: No, Mom…it's Bedwetter B.

Over the course of the season, Bud would be called: Abdomenizer B, Bass Master B, Bedwetter B, Bellringer B, Bushwacker B, Butt-wagger B, Court Jester B, Crossdresser B, Dustbuster B, Gaspasser B, Ghostbuster B, Grand Bastard B, Grand Flasher B, Grandmaster Virgin, Grasshopper B, Mixmaster B, Thighmaster B, and more.

Bud's new high school image aside, there was one episode in Season 6, "Rites of Passage," that forged the father-son bond Bud had always craved with Al. Rites of passage are a common subject on family sitcoms, where parents help kids with their first kiss, first date, first job, and first everything else. On *Married… With Children*, however, Bud, had no expectations that Al would even acknowledge his eighteenth birthday, no less memorialize it, which is why Bud is overcome with pride when Al announces:

AL: I'm taking you to the nudie bar.

BUD: Oh, Dad. I knew you loved me.

AL: Yes, the nudie bar…(SINGS) Where the music stinks, and they water the drinks. The nudie bar, where the girlies dance in their underpants, the nudie bar.

It isn't until after the initial thrills of being at The Jiggly Room wear off, however, that Al reveals that the real rite of passage into manhood he had in mind for Bud had nothing to do with putting dollar bills in stripper's G-strings. Instead, it was the

Bundy family tradition of the bar fight, which Al then purpose-fully ignites by picking a fistfight with an unsuspecting gawker. This leads to Al and Bud bonding over the uncanny teamwork they display in the ensuing brawl where they break a chair over someone's back, a bottle over someone's head, and fight their way to Bundy father-son glory.

> **AL:** Eighteen years old and your first bar fight, like every other male Bundy before you. I'm proud of you son. How do you feel?

> **BUD:** I feel great, Dad. But where do we tell Mom we went in the morning?

> **AL:** Well, son, you're a man now. You stare her straight in the eye, and you tell her we were stuck in traffic. But we know where we were. (SINGS) The nudie bar, where you *can't* touch a breast, but you *can* cave in a chest at the nudie bar. Where you can look at a thigh, and blacken an eye at the nudie bar. Where the beer gives you gas but the Bundys kick ass at the nudie bar.

Gerry Cohen, who directed the episode, said that it was a landmark for the show because "It was our first time that Al and Bud were standing back to back and staving off the world." Gerry also noted a significant parallel *off-camera* development as well: "Ed took David under his arm during this period and tutored him on how to believe in his character's point of view and that he didn't need to push too hard. David totally bought into that and was able to emulate Ed's strengths in that area. They were often sitting on the couch on stage together during rehearsal and they would go back and forth with the material and Eddie was incredibly generous with David and it was exceptionally helpful. David adored the attention from Ed."

David, who started the show when he was only thirteen, confirmed this. "The older I got, the harder it was to shake my nerves and perform. And whenever I was having a problem, Ed would pull me aside and encourage me, always telling me: 'You're the boss. You're the boss.'"

Jefferson D'Arcy also fills out his role this season. "My biggest issue with the character, at first," Ted told me, "is that I didn't like that they matched me to Marcy. I felt at some point they had to make Jefferson a man, so he and Al could work together. That's why they made him a secret agent." Now he mainly used his shady skills to con Marcy into thinking he was serious about finding a job when in fact he was more than content to live on her largess and her sexual attraction to him.

When I asked Ted what it was like to replace an icon like Steve, Ted said, "I didn't *replace* Steve. We were very different and the way Al reacted to us was different. It had to be. David Garrison was so good that he would have stayed there forever if he hadn't wanted to go."

The end of the season gave rise to *Married* satirizing the long-standing tradition where sitcom families take vacations to lush tropical islands or glamorous domestic destinations like Hollywood or Disney World. The antisitcom Bundys end up winning an all-expenses vacation to the English Village of Lower Uncton. After they get there, however, they discover the trip was really a ruse by the townsfolk who can only lift a centuries-old curse on the dreary, cloud-covered village if they rid the world of the remaining male Bundys, meaning Al and Bud.

During a short stay in London, where the Bundys prove to be just as boorish as they are at home, the family departs for Lower Uncton where unbeknownst to them, the male Bundys are marked for murder. After various near-miss attempts on Al and Bud's lives, Al is challenged to a one-on-one battle to the death, in a medieval joust, which he accepts with a rousing, "*Let's joust.*" He ultimately wins by compensating for his lack of skills on horseback with his legendary skills at football. Al and Bud's lives are saved and the curse on the village is lifted.

This three-part family vacation was not considered *Married's* finest hour but, true to the series' original mission, it was a very different take on traditional sitcoms, right down to the titles: 1, "England Show," 2, "Wastin' the Company's Money," and 3, "We're Spending as Fast as We Can."

Christina Applegate and David Faustino may have assumed bigger roles in the series in Season 6, but it was Amanda Bearse who made the most significant career move on the show, though it had nothing to do with her portrayal of Marcy D'Arcy. While negotiating her contract at the end of Season 5, Amanda asked for a shot at directing an episode of the series and Ron and Michael generously agreed to let her have this big opportunity.

"I took directing classes at the American Film Institute and USC," Amanda said "so that I could be more prepared for the job. I had also worked under and observed many directors to learn what to do, or not to do."

Amanda Bearse did such a good job for Ron and Michael they awarded her another episode to direct later in Season 6 and, before the series ended, she directed over thirty episodes and established a new career for herself.

When asked about going the extra mile for Amanda when she wanted to direct or Katey when she was pregnant, Michael said: "Any behavior toward the staff and cast may be summed up simply in that we were a team. As trite as that may seem and as generic a Hollywood response as it sounds, it's how Ron and I truly regarded our 'family.'

"Personally, I was an adopted child and for the first several years, I was the only adopted child. Not only do I believe this may have contributed to any creative facet I possess (simply because I had no sibling to talk to or to learn from so I made them up) but it also fostered a lifelong desire to become part of a 'real' family that you could depend on to have your back no matter what the situation.

"Later on, this desire morphed into becoming to be part of team. An equal. Unfortunately, I came along bereft of athletic ability, which ruled out sports, or musical prowess, which ruled out becoming a Temptation. You'd think my foray into situation comedies would finally help fulfill this desire to but it didn't take long to realize that both ego and the lust for power totally superseded any desires among many of my peers for actual teamwork. That is until *Married.*

"Ron and I ran the show differently. There wasn't much of a hierarchy. We didn't believe that someone wasn't 'worthy' to stand in another teammate's shadow. We never wanted any staff member to be 'afraid' to come speak to us. If a crew member would suggest a joke they felt it was better than what we'd written, we'd gladly accept it if they were right.

"Since FOX paid our staff less than the established networks, we would hand out 'promotions' that would automatically increase their pay scale. It wasn't just a matter of being magnanimous (although sometimes it was), but we truly felt these were 'our people,' they were good at their jobs and most of them stuck with us from the beginning when they could've easily gone to work on a *real* network for more money. So we pretty much *owed* them for their loyalty."

In return, Ron and Michael inspired an almost obsessive dedication to them. For example, one day Marti Squyres, whom they had early on promoted to wardrobe supervisor, was crossing Ventura Boulevard with her arms full of packages of clothing she had just purchased for that week's show. As she crossed the street, she was obsessing over all the items she still needed to buy when she was stabbed in the chest by two men who stole her purse and ran away.

Marti, bleeding and enraged, ran after her attackers until a passerby tried to convince her that even if she caught the thieves, they would only do more harm to her. "But those guys stole my purse with my credit cards," Marti insisted, "and I have got to go shopping for the show!" Marti was eventually persuaded to call the police (and her husband), and managed to tend to her wounds and finish the rest of her shopping in time for the production. "It wasn't the smartest thing I've ever done," she admitted, "but if I had to do it all over again I'd do the same thing. 'Cause that's all I cared about." Obviously, not everyone on the show was put to the same test as Marti, but her actions were symbolic of how almost everyone viewed Ron and Michael.

Marti, Katey, and Amanda are just a few of examples of how Michael and Ron turned what I sometimes experienced on other shows as a cold, cutthroat, every-person-for-them-self environment into a family atmosphere that for most people was the best job of their lives. But just as families are known to work together for the common good, they are also known to foster petty jealousies and acting-out behaviors that can severely test those bonds. The *Married... With Children* family would prove to be no exception to that rule.

POSTSCRIPT—THE NUDIE BAR—WHERE THE MUSIC STINKS AND THEY WATER THE DRINKS

The nudie bar was to Al Bundy what Moe's Tavern was to Homer Simpson, Central Perk was to *Friends*, and Bada Bing! was to Tony Soprano. "We created the nudie bar to give Al an outside life, a place to go," Moye said. "Clearly Al wouldn't do anything but sit there and probably get hammered and appreciate what he saw. After a while it became a temple to him. The world is *right*, now. This is where I can be at peace."

Considering how closely the nudie bar came to be associated with *Married... With Children*, although it was mentioned in Season 4, Al never actually goes there until Season 6. After that, we only go there six more times in the entire series. Its inflated impression is, no doubt, due to how it manages to provide a higher degree of titillation in an already titillating series, and also how seamlessly the nudie bar amplifies both the positives and negatives in Al's life.

For example, in Season 9's "The Naked and the Dead, but Mostly the Naked," Peggy, Marcy and their girlfriends disparage Al and his buddies for going to the strip club because "They're saying, you don't turn us on anymore, so we'll just get stimulated elsewhere." As they all agree how low their men have stooped in sexualizing women in this way, Marcy clutches a picture of John F. Kennedy Jr. and immediately works herself into a shuddering orgasm.

Meanwhile, when confronted, Al and the guys swear to their wives that the nudie bar has nothing to do with them lusting after women but is simply a place to "relax and unwind." This, however, backfires as the women consequently demand they take them to the nudie bar to prove just how "relaxing" and "innocent" it really is. When the guys and their wives get to The Jiggly Room, the men convincingly manage to tamp down their base instincts for a short while, ordering mineral water and discussing the merits of "health care reform." Then, however, one particular stripper, Rocky Mountains, performs in a way that makes the guys lose control and suddenly start dancing with the other strippers in the club as their wives look on aghast.

The guys realize they've blown it and have to find a way to make it up to their women. Then we cut to the outside of each of their houses, where we hear the voices of each wife calling out their husband's name in pleasure: "Oh, Ike!" "Oh, Bob Rooney!" "Oh, Al!"

In "Turning Japanese," Marcy is up for a big promotion with her bank, Kyoto National. After several failed attempts to impress the president of the bank, Mr. Shimokowa (Pat Morito), they both end up at The Jiggly Room where she abandons all of her stated principles and does a wild striptease that pleases Mr. Shimokowa and ultimately lands her the job.

In Season 11's "Twisted," when the Bundys and the D'Arcys take shelter from a tornado in the Bundys basement, we reveal that Al and Jefferson have tunneled a secret underground passage that leads from the Bundy shelter into the middle of the nudie bar.

"Live Nude Peg" finds Peggy so jealous that Al is spending so much time ogling women at the nudie bar, she disguises herself as an exotic dancer and wins the Amateur Night contest as Jasmine. Al, who is in the audience, is so turned on by Jasmine, (whom he doesn't recognize as Peggy), he goes home and fantasizes about her while having the best sex with Peggy ever…fantasizing about her as Jasmine, while we all know it is really Peggy. A win-win for the Bundys.

Little known facts about the nudie bar, gleaned from signs on the wall:

- A-Cup Night on Thursdays
- Amateur Night on Tuesdays
- Full Price Night on Fridays
- Foreign Exchange Day
- Eight Drink Minimum

A lot of the positive fan reaction to the nudie bar also came from the nudie bar songs that Al and the guys robustly break into whenever the subject of the nudie bar comes to mind.

> Yes, the nudie bar!
> Where the music stinks
> and they water the drinks
> The nudie bar
> Where the girls dance
> in their underpants
> The nudie bar

MARRIED... WITH CHILDREN VS THE WORLD

Where you see a butt
and their trap stays shut
At the nudie bar
where you can look at a thigh
and blacken an eye
At the nudie bar!
Where the beer gives you gas,
but the Bundys kick ass
Where a buck's enough
to see their stuff
At the nudie bar!
Where the breasts may be fake
but man, do they shake
At the nudie bar!
Where you swear like a sailor
and wish you could nail her
At the nudie bar!
Where the cops are at the door
and there's a Kennedy on the floor
At the nudie bar!
To the nudie bar!
Where Christmas is nice
And lap dancers are half price
At the nudie bar!
Where you drink down the shooters
And unwrap the hooters
At the nudie bar!
Where eggnog's a-plenty
And the girls are all twenty
At the nudie bar!

A much tamer, but no less graphic representation of Al's sexual fantasy life is the running joke about his favorite magazine, *Big 'Uns*. The publication having been founded by one Flint Guccione (a play on *Penthouse*'s real publisher, Bob Guccione), with the convergence of *an* Instamatic, a drunken family reunion, and fifty bucks. Al uses *Big 'Un's* the same way he uses the nudie bar—as an escape from the grim reminders of his everyday life. Also featured are offshoots of *Big 'Uns—Colossal 'Uns, Black 'Uns* and, from Cuba, *Cub 'Uns*.

CHAPTER 13

SEASON 7: WHO'S THE BOSS?

BY THE TIME SEASON 7 rolled around, Michael Moye had tired of the day-to-day demands of running *Married... With Children* and decided to dissolve his long-term partnership with Ron Leavitt to work on his own projects as a solo writer. Ron, meanwhile, with the studio and network's blessing, made a deal to stay on the series as its sole showrunner.

Adding to any uncertainty this shift might have created with the cast and crew about how the show was going to run this year was the perception that comedy writers who work together as a team do so because they have personal strengths and weaknesses that are compensated for by their partners. In this scenario, one writer is the *story person* who knows how to cleverly structure a narrative but wouldn't know a joke if it exploded in his (or her) pants. The other partner is the *joke machine* who couldn't string together a coherent chronicle of the last five minutes but could come up with a big laugh whenever the story calls for it, and even better, when it doesn't.

One journalist, looking back at the different phases of *Married... With Children*, even went so far as to conclude that Leavitt was the story guy, "counterbalancing raunchiness to center many stories on the relationships shared between the core characters." Moye, on the other hand, was the "funny guy, knowing how to imbue a script with a laugh-a-minute rhythm that could make even an adequate story appear better."

I can tell you with certainty, however, from years of experience, working together and separately with Ron and Michael, that they were both *funny-story guys*, more than capable of running our show, or any show for that matter, on their own. The cast and the crew, on the other hand, had only known Ron and Michael as a team, on a show that required a lot of teamwork, and as much as they had come to love and trust them together, they understandably had no idea what to expect from either of them as individual entities.

Amanda Bearse was philosophical: "We were lucky to have Ron and Michael together, but they divorced as writers. Things do shift." "Daddy and Daddy broke up," she added, aptly driving the family metaphor home. Amanda was right. We had been a very close *family* both on and off the screen, who had gone through a lot together and even the most amicable divorces can take their toll on the *kids*. Though everyone was willing to give Ron the benefit of the doubt, I could sense that the forthcoming year was going to be a wait-and-see situation.

Long before there was time to wait *or* see, however, another major decision was made that promised to create another disruptive change within the *Married* family and it had nothing to do with Ron and Michael splitting up. We, they, or someone decided to add a six-year-old boy to the cast as a regular character in the Bundy household. We were, in a manner of speaking, losing a parent and gaining a child at the same time.

"*Married... With Children*," Mara Reinstein wrote in her introduction to the series when it started streaming on Hulu, "didn't just push the envelope, it ripped the envelope apart, burned it and threw the remains into the wind." For all the new ground the series broke in its first six years, however, in Season 7 we had somehow turned to one of the oldest sitcom tropes ever, adding a new character—a sweet, innocent six-year-old child named Seven.

The new character gambit is a common ploy used to pump up interest in long running sitcoms and in some cases, it can work incredibly well, like when *Friends* added Mike Hannigan (Paul Rudd) or *Curb Your Enthusiasm* added Leon Black (J. B. Smoove). You could even argue that *Cheers* adding Woody (Woody Harrelson), and then Rebecca (Kirstie Alley), actually made the show better and allowed them to stay fresh for another six seasons. *Married*'s own cast members would later prove to be very successful as *new characters* added to other series, as when *Friends* added Christina Applegate or when Ed O'Neill was brought on to *West Wing* or when Katey Sagal was, ironically, hired to play Dan's wife on *The Conners* after Roseanne had left the show.

"The problem with adding Seven," however, according to an article on the website, *TV Tropes* "was how *Married... With Children* relied on a lot of adult, sexual and sadistic humor that really didn't work with a child and writing jokes appropriate for him clashed with the usual tone of the show." With all the choices available for adding a character—friend, neighbor, boss, love interest, it's fair to ask how did *Married*—the raunchy anti-sitcom—land on adopting a sweet, six-year-old child?

RICHARD GURMAN

Michael Moye speculated that, though FOX may have begun as an *outlier* network, with *Married... With Children*'s growing popularity and the growing ratings and demographic strength of *The Simpsons, Beverly Hills, 90210*, and *In Living Color*, it was becoming a legitimate rival to the Big Three. "Now that they were beginning to emerge as a *real* network," Moye concluded, "they started thinking like a *real* network and thought bringing in Seven was a good idea—and it wasn't."

Regardless of who was to blame, after several awkward episodes when it became clear that Seven wasn't working at all, we cut his screen time to the bones until halfway through the season he finally disappeared from the Bundy household without any explanation. "The funniest thing about that kid," O'Neill recalls, "was fourteen episodes later when Bud opened up the refrigerator and Seven's photo appeared on a missing child announcement on the side of a milk carton." The only thing that seemed like a stretch about that joke was that Peggy had actually bought milk for her family.

In spite of the negative audience and critical reaction to Seven, critic Jackson Upperco, noted, "Seven is the year's anachronism, not its ambassador, appearing in only twelve of the first eighteen episodes. Of those twelve, he's only a major participant in two of the stories. So the year's reputation as being overly burdened by an irritating kid is very much exaggerated."

One episode that actually benefited from having Seven in the family and played nicely on one of Al's strongest fantasies was, "Al On the Rocks." In order to pay Seven's doctor bills, Al thinks he's found the perfect job as a bartender at one of his favorite places, a topless bar, only to have his dreams of getting paid to watch topless women dance shattered when he discovers that the job is actually for *him* to be the topless bartender in a women-only club where *he* would be the one being ogled by them. Eventually, Al embraces the role and does a memorable, Tom Cruise–like bartending bit, shaking cocktails while dancing topless with a bow tie. Al now basks in the glory of the flip side of his fantasies—becoming a sex object to the women at the bar—until, as usual, he ends up the loser when Jefferson gets a bartending job there too and the ogling women reject the shoe man in favor of his hulky gigolo neighbor.

Another memorable episode in Season 7 was "Peggy and the Pirates," an elaborate period costume fantasy piece on a pirate ship that featured the return of David Garrison as Rubio the Cruel. It allowed David to showcase his singing and dancing chops, and for us to mercilessly mock them to the delight of the audience, which welcomed *Steve* back with a sustained ovation.

As broad as *Married... With Children* had become, there was one running gag that originated this season that was inspired by an all-too-true real-life incident. Frank Lloyd, our stunt coordinator who specialized in staging fake but realistic looking fights, came out of Ron Leavitt's house with Ron one afternoon to see that his pickup truck had just been stolen and was making a getaway down the street. Ron and Frank gave chase in Ron's car until they caught up to the stolen truck at a stoplight where Frank got out, dragged the thief out of the driver's seat by his ear and beat the living crap out of him. Ron, who had only seen Frank stage *fake* fights, marveled, "Wow that stuff really works."

Ron, who as we've seen, had a knack for finding the funny in almost any situation, incorporated the incident into an episode of *Married… With Children* when Al finds Kelly snuggling on the couch with a boyfriend and drags him by his ear out the door, bashing his head in along the way. To underscore the cartoonishness of the show's violence (and distinguish it from Frank's), we wrote this exchange:

> **GUY:** Well, I can see by the stars on the wall that it's time to go. See ya, Kelly.
>
> **KELLY:** Thanks a lot, Dad. Now I'll never know his name.

Speaking of cartoonish violence and Kelly's boyfriends, Season 7's "Movie Show" is centered around the simple, but relatable activity of taking your entire family out for a night at the movies, but it eventually evolves into a vehicle for *Married* to reinforce how much Al really loves his kids…and, as it turns out, his fists. After the movie starts, Kelly finds her current boyfriend cheating on her with another girl in the back of the darkened theater, which prompts a brief father-daughter exchange you're not likely to hear on any other family sitcom:

> **KELLY:** Daddy, beat him up.
>
> **AL:** Of course, Pumpkin.

"I start towards him walking fast," Ed recalls. "As soon as I see his reaction, like 'oh, fuck,' and he starts to try to get out of the seat, I go faster at him, almost like a lion attack. Then I really go in hard because I didn't give him a chance to get out of his seat. Then it's just—kill him. And that's what I loved so much about the show. It was brutal, but funny." Fortunately for the series, so was Ed O'Neill.

Of all the episodes we wrote that serve to test Al and Peggy's unbreakable bond, Season 7's "The Proposition" was the most convincing. Al's old girlfriend, Coco, played by *Wheel of Fortune*'s Vanna White, shows up in Chicago still so deeply crushing on Al that she offers to *buy* him from Peggy and the family for $500,000. Peggy doesn't need much persuading at first (nor does Al) and she takes the check for a half a million dollars and immediately starts shopping for a new home with the kids. Eventually, however, when Peggy comes back and finds Al and Coco in bed, she just can't stand the idea of being apart from her man (or seeing him happy), so she gives Coco her money back (though she first tries to cheat her) and throws her out, which sets the scene for a *heartfelt* reconciliation, Bundy style.

> **PEGGY:** Gee, Al, I hope you're not mad at me. I just couldn't stand the thought of you with someone else. Even if it meant we were gonna get rich.
>
> **AL:** I guess I couldn't be with anybody else either, Peg, even though she had more to offer than you in every possible way.
>
> **PEGGY:** Well, I guess we're just meant to be together, huh?
>
> **AL:** Yeah, I guess.
>
> **PEGGY:** You know what I want to do right now?
>
> **AL:** Yes, I do and it's exactly what I want to do.

They shut off the lights and turn to go to sleep. After a beat…

AL: Gee, I can still feel ya, Peg.

PEGGY: I love you, Al.

AL: Yeah, thanks.

Amanda Bearse would direct three episodes this season and continue to excel on both sides of the camera, but as she got more deeply into her role as director, there started to be a shift in attitudes with some players on the set. "What was tough," Ted McGinley remembers, "what was weird was, all of a sudden she was the boss."

"When she first started directing," Ed O'Neill recalls, "I went to the rest of the cast and I said—'Let's really go out of our way to make sure Amanda's experience is great.' But Amanda, at that particular time," according to Ed, "was very touchy. She could be appreciative by the effort by the cast, then if something went wrong, she could get a little prickly, you know. Nothing major." Nothing *major* at the time, but it foreshadowed a feud between the two actors that at times was far more hostile (and much less funny) than the characters they portrayed on the screen.

"I got caught in the middle of all that," Ted remembers. "To try not to come down on one side or the other but having to work with everybody. That's hard. That's just the life of these things. You become like family and as shows get older, wheels get a little wobbly."

The wheels did indeed get wobbly, but they didn't come off the bus…yet. In fact, whatever problems Ed had with Amanda here in Season 7 had no bearing on how he stood up for her when she came up against the outside world, which in one instance prompted Ed O'Neill to take a page right out of Al Bundy's *you can fuck with me but don't fuck with my family* playbook

The *outside world* in this case was represented by Tony Danza, whose rehearsal hall for his ABC hit comedy series *Who's the Boss?* was right next door to our rehearsal hall where we often rehearsed at the same time. One day, "Amanda came out into the hallway between the two halls after rehearsing a particularly loud scene," and, according to Sony senior vice president Fran McConnell, "Danza came running out because it was disturbing them and started screaming at Amanda to shut up. Tony was playing— this is *my* show, I'm the *patron*. Then Ed came charging out of *Married... With Children*'s rehearsal hall and grabbed Tony by his shirt and said—'You don't talk to anybody on my show like that.' Tony backed down and that was the end of it." But it fairly raises the question posed by the title of Tony's series, *Who's the Boss?*

POSTSCRIPT—KELLY AND HER FAMOUS "ISMS"

Kelly Bundy may have started the series as a girl of average intelligence, but her rapid descent into ditziness scored such huge points with the audience it became one of the most popular features of the series. Playing stupid is nothing new for a sitcom character, but what distinguished Kelly Bundy from the rest of the sitcom pack, was the unexpected intelligence and off center logic that informed her seemingly mindless commentary.

KELLY: What time is it?

BUD: (CHECKING HIS WATCH) Three thirty.

KELLY: A.M. or B.M.?

BUD: B.M.

KELLY: You know, I don't know why they call it B.M. Why don't they call it P.M. for post meridian?

In this speech, ostensibly about her health, her diagnosis is muddy but her intent is transparent.

KELLY: Hi, Daddy. I just wanted to tell you I just got a call from the doctor, and I'm dying. I've got Bulgaria. The doctor says that it's terminus. I've got 'til Christmas morning, and the only known cure is a good present.

In an episode where Al is enraged over a rabbit who is eating all the carrots he planted and decides to use a shotgun to solve the problem, Kelly draws on her many hours of research to warn her father off this approach.

KELLY: Daddy, let me give you some advice. Um, I've been watching these television shows about rabbits. Don't put the barrel of the gun down the hole. Because what they'll do is that they'll tie it in a knot so that it explodes in your face. Or sometimes what they'll do is they make it really long and curved so that it comes up in a hole behind you and you'll shoot yourself in the butt.

When Kelly expresses what seems like an ill-founded fear about how her father will embarrass himself when speaking to the city council, she makes a point that may be hard to understand but is impossible to refute.

KELLY: I just hope he doesn't make a testicle out of himself.

PEGGY: You mean "spectacle," honey.

KELLY: No, I mean "testicle." I'm used to the spectacle thing.

And this Kellyism makes perfect sense but still gives you pause.

KELLY: Those who can do; those who can't do not.

The real secret to Kelly's success with this character trait, however, wasn't the writing, but Christina Applegate herself. "I don't think we knew initially how talented she truly was," Gerry Cohen, who directed her more than anyone, observed. "She played that character off of one simple principle—believe at all times that you are the smartest person in the room. There wasn't any self-awareness that she might not know something or that she might not be correct. And that was Christina's key to making Kelly so funny."

"She not only looked the part," Michael Moye added to Gerry's point, "but could also *act* the part."

Aside from Kelly's long-winded bits, she chalked up an abundance of highlights on YouTube and other internet sites with very short bursts of what have become known as "Kellyisms."

KELLY: As inevitable as death in Texas.

KELLY: Comme ci, comme di.

KELLY: Squid pro quo.

KELLY: Strip-search me.

KELLY: E before O, except before E-I-E-I-O

KELLY: In a buttshell.

KELLY: G-Spot (for ten-spot)

KELLY: Mental pause (menopause)

KELLY: Monte Cristo's revenge

KELLY: Stereo system (stereotype)

KELLY: Topeka! (eureka)

KELLY: I'm on the horns of an enema.

CHAPTER 14

SEASON 8: JUMPING THE SHARK, COMING OUT OF THE CLOSET, AND OTHER ACTS OF COURAGE

AFTER MARRIED SUCCESSFULLY ADJUSTED TO losing Michael Moye in Season 7, Season 8 would be Ron Leavitt's year to leave the show to work on his own projects, so the revolving door turned once again and Michael walked back in from outside to run the show. Michael, as Ron did before him, would turn out to be an inspiring writer and a terrific showrunner on his own. Michael's stewardship, however, would turn out to be only one of many subplots in the backstage drama that would capture the headlines in *Married... With Children*'s eighth season as the line between the Bundy family saga and our real-life work-family story continued to blur.

In an early episode of Season 8, while Marcy D'Arcy the otherwise uptight, yuppie banker was amusing our audience (and nauseating Al) with vivid, over-the-top accounts of her sexual prowess with men—

> **MARCY:** During sex, I talk, yell, scream...Oh yes, yes. Oh, Jefferson! Oh Steve! Oh, Jamal!

—Amanda Bearse, the living, breathing human being was telling a very different story to an equally captivated audience in a cover story in the LGBTQ+ newsmagazine *The Advocate* where she came out as a lesbian.

"They had been outing Amanda Bearse for years in the tabloids," according to Judy Wieder, editor of *The Advocate*. "She had been coping with the decision of coming out for quite some time. What happened was they got wind of the fact that she and her girlfriend decided to adopt a baby."

"That's when I made the decision," Amanda said, "that there's nothing negative about me and my life, my choices, my child… all of those things that deserve respect and integrity. There was never any shame for me about being gay. That's when I decided to tell the story *my* way, and yes everybody was supportive.

"I had been living my life *out*," Amanda noted, "so that was the professional move. Everybody knew I was gay on the set. I mean it wasn't a big secret or anything. I was the first person in prime-time television—male or female—to come out of the closet,"

"She laid all the groundwork for others," Wieder pointed out. "You have to remember that Amanda did this before Melissa Etheridge did it, before Chastity Bono did it, before Greg Louganis did it. As a TV star she probably paved the way for Ellen DeGeneres to consider whether or not she could risk doing that," which she did, four years later.

"We were all thinking," Ted McGinley remembers, "good for her and just let her live her life and I think it made things much easier for her."

"Not everybody is as fortunate as I am to have had that kind of support," Amanda recalls. "*Married* understood who I was as

Amanda, but they also wrote a wonderful character for me to portray and I love Marcy. She's dear to me and they saw me as a competent enough actress that it didn't matter. It was a rich experience to feel the support...it was more like it was a nonissue."

Michael Moye, who fully embraced Amanda's decision, acknowledged, however, that it wasn't totally a "nonissue." There was some "concern" in some quarters that her coming out might negatively impact the ratings, "but nobody was really panicked. It was just, how is the audience going to buy the marriage between her and Ted? In the end, once again, the audience proved that they know they were just watching a show...they're not taking this seriously."

Meanwhile, as we turned to our main mission of actually making a TV show, Season 8 produced some of the funniest episodes of the entire series run while simultaneously delivering others that represented the last toehold the show had on it's already tenuous grasp on reality. This grip had been slowly slipping away since Season 5, but now as Amanda Bearse observed, "the character of Al Bundy was increasingly conceived of as Wile E. Coyote. That's how we were treating the *reality* as the years went on."

This type of exaggerated storytelling, to one degree or another, occurs so predictably in the sunset years of any long-running comedy, that there's even a name for it—*Jumping the Shark*—coined for an episode from the fifth season of *Happy Days* where Fonzie literally jumps over a shark while on water skis. These surreal, pandering-for-ratings stunts have come to signify the precise moment when a show has passed its peak, and from which it rarely rebounds, though *Happy Days* went on to enjoy six more highly rated seasons.

Even a sophisticated show like *Cheers*, which won twenty-eight Emmys, wasn't immune to the jump. In its Season 8, a psychic held a séance in the bar to conjure up Carla's husband, Eddie, from the dead. In Season 11 of *Frasier*, Dr. Crane has a nightmare in which he kills Niles and marries Daphne. *Friends* jumps the shark in Season 5 when Ross is at the altar about to marry Emily and utters "I take thee, Rachel," instead of "I take thee, Emily," during his vows.

Though Season 8 of *Married… With Children* can be seen as its obvious "shark" season, it's important to point out that from day one, *Married* shouldered the burden of (as well as reveled in the pleasure of) portraying outrageous, over-the-top characters as part of its disruptive, satirical agenda. The cumulative result for our audience was that watching our characters outlandish and boundary-breaking behavior eventually "normalized," their "abnormalities," challenging us to push those borders out even further to deliver a "new abnormal."

Complicating our task was that, by Season 8, the type of traditional TV series we originally set out to mock—*Cosby, Family Ties, Growing Pains, Full House*—was disappearing, replaced by edgier shows like *Frasier, Beavis and Butt-Head, Grace Under Fire, Martin, Roseanne, Roc, In Living Color, Seinfeld*, and *The Simpsons*. *Married… With Children* no doubt helped cause some of these stylistic shifts; nonetheless, we were still competing for ratings and it was hard to keep your promise to be different than the other networks when the other networks were being different too.

Married took some of the curse off of this *cartoony* bent by being self-aware and even calling attention to our own heightened sense of reality. For example, in "High I.Q.," when Al and Jefferson try to get a blow torch to work by holding a lighter to the barrel, Peggy says:

PEGGY: Wow. You can almost hear the *Looney Tunes* theme, can't you?

You almost could, as in the next beat the blow torch exploded and burned off Al's eyebrows.

"Wabbit Season," can be seen as actually embracing *cartoonism*. In the episode Al, a la Elmer Fudd, tries to kill a "wascally wabbit," which is pulling up the vegetables Al planted in his new garden. Al ends up shooting himself in one foot with a shotgun, the other with a flamethrower, and then blowing up the neighborhood by accidentally putting dynamite next to a gas main. If this wasn't an obvious enough ode to *Looney Toons*, the episode ends with Peggy framed in a cartoon iris, spouting Porky Pig's signature chuckling cartoon sign-off: "Th-th that's all, folks."

However, these episodes are Ken Burns documentaries compared to Season 8's "How Green Was My Apple," where, "We didn't just jump the shark," as Michael Moye put it, "we were pole vaulting the ocean." The story involves a dispute over a property line that causes the Bundys and the D'Arcys to have a classic Hatfields-versus-McCoys feud. This vendetta includes Jefferson brandishing a shotgun, Al jacking up one entire side of the D'Arcy house on an angle so steep it sends their furniture sliding against the wall, and Jefferson retaliating by launching a rocket that knocks out the side of the Bundy house. Just to remind the audience that we were still satirizing traditional family programming, we also stuck in appearances by historic sitcom icons Gary Coleman (*Diff'rent Strokes*) and Danny Bonaduce (*Partridge Family*) whose bits were to deny they were the stars we know them to be.

"A Little Off the Top" asked the audience to buy that Al's doctors misread his surgical instructions to give him a *circular incision*, and instead gave him a *circumcision*...ouch! The visual payoff to this bit was (no, not a swollen penis, though that was pitched in the writers' room) a hospital ward full of newly circumcised baby boys wailing in their cribs with Al in a crib next to them, crying like a baby.

Season 8 saw another Buck-driven-Cheech-Marin-voiced episode, which, though it wanders into surreal territory, is grounded in relatable feelings of a family member who feels neglected; a family member who is also well versed in the cynical humor of his owners.

> **BUCK:** Hey, don't mind me. I'll just lick my genitalia and go to sleep alone. Much like the boy. Ha ha ha. Hey, ever hear of affection? We love to be petted Much like the girl. Ah, well, that's it. I'm fed up. I can takes no more. I'm outta here.

Buck runs away again and this time ends up in the dog pound where he will be gassed in a week if no one claims him. The Bundys, oblivious at first, come to the rescue just in time to save their beloved but often ignored pet and, in its own twisted way, validate Buck as a true member of the Bundy family.

This year, even the already broad rivalry between Al and Marcy takes a sharklike leap with the formation of Al's ad hoc group, NO MA'AM (National Organization of Men Against Amazonian

Masterhood), and the group that Marcy forms to counter their influence, "F.A.N.G." (Feminists Against Neanderthal Guys).

The origin of Al's group comes in the eponymous episode, "NO MA'AM," where Al and his buddies, Bob Rooney (played by E. E. Bell), Officer Dan (played by Dan Tullis Jr.), and Jefferson are angered that their regular bowling night was cancelled in favor of a Women's League. They are further enraged when they decide to go to the nudie bar instead, only to learn that their favorite strip club has been turned into a feminist poetry club.

When they discover that this has all been orchestrated by Marcy and her feminist friends, it drives Al to form NO MA'AM. "Political correctness was really getting a foothold into everything," Michael Moye said, "and we thought we've got to send this up." To that end, NO MA'AM's first official act was to storm a live, Jerry Springer–type daytime talk show, *The Masculine Feminist*, gamely played by Jerry Springer himself. NO MA'AM ties Jerry up and performs a "sexorcism" by forcing him to watch a pro wrestling match on TV in front of his audience.

For all of its crazy public antics, when NO MA'AM held its meetings, all they did was drink beer, pee, drink more beer, and assign crazy initiation rites, like buying a pair of panty shields in broad daylight. "I thought it was a great to have those meetings in the Bundy garage," Ed recalls. "It was very much like when I was a Cub Scout in my neighborhood, and all the kids were basically juvenile delinquents. We'd eat snacks and watch *Davey Crockett* on TV and we weren't really accomplishing anything as Cub Scouts. We were getting together just to fuck around. Just like NO MA'AM."

When NO MA'AM did spring into action, however, it took on some issues that deeply resonated with our core audience. For example, the members protested the real 1994 baseball players' strike by forming baseball teams of their own to play in major-league stadiums in front of grateful fans who were tired of being denied their favorite sport by greedy pro athletes and billion-aire owners.

Marcy herself *jumps the shark* in "Banking on Marcy," when she employs a new-age technique called "transference" to conquer her fear of public speaking. This fantasy-based exercise succeeds in banishing her fear of speaking in public, but the *solution*—pretending you're in a more relaxed situation, like the bedroom—leads to her having a convulsive orgasm on stage while giving a speech to a group of bankers. Many sitcoms have tackled the problem of fear of public speaking, but, none to my knowledge have proffered our solution.

As broad and cartoonish as the episodes in Season 8 became, "Hood 'n' the Boyz" was steeped in core Bundy values. In this story, Al stands up for an old girlfriend against a gang of young hoodlums who are harassing her at her convenience store. Here, Al explains to the gang leader Ray Ray (Matt Borlenghi), who has already soundly kicked Al's ass twice, why he keeps coming back to defend her.

> **AL:** I'm a moron, Ray Ray. That's what comes from being a man. From the first worm they dare us to eat to the last shovelful of snow they convince us we can move, we're nothing more to women than an amusement park ride with life insurance. For example...You ski? No. Well, you will someday if a girl wants you to.

We all will. We'd hurtle down that mountain so fast that the crack of our bodies hitting the tree wouldn't even resonate in their ears before we'd pounce up and say, "I'm okay." And we've all been to a weight room when a pretty girl walks by and said to ourselves, "Gee, I think I'll start today's warm-up bench press with, oh, nine tons." So you see, Ray Ray, as long as there's women, there'll be men around doing stupid things to impress them. Now, someday you may evolve beyond this, but it's too late for me. I'm too old…too married. So either I split so you look cool in front of your girl, or you look cool in front of yours and kill me. Let's rock.

POSTSCRIPT—SEX IN CAPTIVITY

Sex, like sports, was a major theme in *Married… With Children* except, instead being used simply to relive the glory days of now-paunchy middle-aged-men, sex was a theme that touched all parties of all ages and skill levels on the show. "You could argue that the entire series is about sex," observes critic Jackson Upperco. "Peg begs Al for it, Marcy manipulates Steve with it, Jefferson dazzles Marcy with it, Kelly oozes it, Bud lacks it." So many of the guest stars we hired were Playboy Playmates that the Playboy Modeling Agency sent our casting supervisor, Tammy Billick, a free subscription to *Playboy Magazine*. "This came in handy," Tammy said, "because I would often get a call from Ron Leavitt saying, 'Could you please check out, Miss May?'" for the next episode. Eventually, over twenty Playboy Playmates appeared on *Married*, including Pamela Anderson and Shannon Tweed.

Married... With Children's use of Playboy Playmates and voluptuous women was often the target of feminist critiques of the show, but I remember one instance where it was the Playmate herself who crossed over our admittedly thin line. This woman recurred in minor roles in the series and one time when she was on the show we received a barrage of complaints from Katey Sagal, Christina Applegate, and Amanda Bearse that she had been repeatedly flashing everyone on stage during rehearsal.

We obviously had to put a stop to it, so Ron and Michael called the flasher into our executive offices to have a talk. When she arrived, our fearless leaders told her with all the sobriety they could muster, that, although we liked her acting on the screen, her exhibitionism during rehearsals was inappropriate, distracting, and she would have to stop it or be fired. The woman was caught off guard, became uncharacteristically sullen, and hung her head in shame. After a beat she looked up through tearful eyes and said that she understood she could no longer flash people on stage, but would it be alright if she still flashed us. Then, with better comedic timing than she ever displayed on camera, she quickly flashed us and made a perfect exit out the door. As the cliché goes—you can't write this stuff!

Sexual frankness in dialogue and on-screen was an obvious tool to attract attention (and viewers) for the series, but it also attracted its share of criticism. In addition to Terry Rakolta's protest about the general raunchiness of our show relative to our time slot, we also got a lot of pushback about our portrayal of Kelly. Michael Moye scoffed at the idea that, while people were attacking Kelly Bundy they were praising the character of the popular TV attorney on another FOX show, *Ally McBeal* "who as I recall, either fantasized or in reality, would sleep with anyone...you could barely see her, she was buried under men. Kelly, became the example of vulgarity, but you never saw her doing anything untoward. Ally would bang anything and that was an example of *stellar writing*."

Kelly's sexual reputation, was also, as Michael points out, greatly exaggerated, mainly because it was being spread by a very unreliable narrator—her brother.

> **BUD:** Kel, it's seven o'clock, shouldn't you be cuffed to a radiator by now?
>
> **KELLY:** So, how do I look?
>
> **BUD:** Like a limited edition, condom-packin' Barbie.
>
> **KELLY:** He's got a house in Jamaica. Do you know what I would do for a house in Jamaica?
>
> **BUD:** Yeah, the same thing you'd do for dinner and a movie.

Just as often, however, Kelly shot back at Bud's *lack* of sexual prowess, proving, as Amanda Bearse remarked, that in spite of *Married... With Children*'s offensiveness, at least it was "an equal opportunity offender."

> **BUD:** These were noises I never heard before.
>
> **KELLY:** Well, then it could have been a girl moaning your name.
>
> **BUD:** Good news, it's official.
>
> **KELLY:** Ah, the State of Illinois finally recognized the sacred bond between you and your hand.

Or the many times she teases him about his attachment to his plastic blow-up doll, Isis. As when she informs Al about Bud's date.

KELLY: I tell ya…it was a real girl. Honest. There was no blow-up tube in the back or anything.

Or, similarly, when Bud emerges from his room in rare post-coital afterglow with his new girlfriend, Ariel, and Kelly quickly checks the back of her neck and assures the whole family:

KELLY: Nope, no air nozzle.

Kelly certainly flaunts her sexuality and owns having sex on occasion but there were also times when she drew the line against promiscuity and even made a stand against it. In Season 7's "T-R-A-Something-Something Spells Tramp," Kelly is parked in a car in an isolated lovers' lane with a boy, Ralph. When Kelly resists his advances and he finally says, "Put out or get out," Kelly promptly punches him in the face and gets out of the car to walk home.

The "no means no" theme is played out further when, as Kelly's walks home, she runs into two other girls who were also told by their dates to put out or get out, "POOGO," as they call it, and when one of the girls wonders why men call *them* tramps, Kelly responds as only she can:

KELLY: Men are the real tramps. They'll do it for any-one, anytime, anyplace. I was walking home from a date one time through the cemetery, and I heard these people wailing: "Oh Grandpa! Oh Grandpa!" and everybody's weeping and everything. And then I hear this guy go: "Hooters at five o'clock." And so everyone turns to look at me, the pall bearers drop the casket, Grandpa's head comes rolling out—it was a railroad accident—and all the men from the funeral come running up to me, going: "God, I loved Grandpa. Let's do it in his casket." Men are tramps.

Looking back on the series, Christina occasionally spoke out about being portrayed in such a frank sexual manner, but she always tempered it with the idea that the show was satirical and not supposed to be taken seriously. Also, "Because *I* was so different," she told *E! True Hollywood Story* in an extended piece about the show, "I don't think I ever attached myself to the idea of being stereotyped."

For all the sexual explicitness on *Married... With Children*, the sexual issue that defined the Bundy marriage and most satirized the traditional sitcom was *not* having sex.

PEGGY: I want sex.

AL: Well so do I, but I see no reason to drag you into it.

Though Al and Peggy clearly have opposite views about sex with each other, they both have a heavy appetite for sex as a spectator sport: going to strip clubs, reading girlie (and manly) magazines, fantasizing about it, and scoring points about the other's sexual plusses and minuses.

PEGGY: Come on, Al. It's time for you to do your chores.

AL: Wait a second, Peg. We had sex three nights ago. I'm still kind of woozy.

PEGGY: The garbage, Al. The longer of the two jobs.

AL: And the more rewarding.

Despite the sexual minefield, for people to laugh and identify with this bombastic couple, Ron and Michael knew their audience had to be confident Al and Peggy would never leave each other, which is why we shot several episodes where sex is available to one or the other of them, but is ultimately resisted. In "Al Loses His Cherry," after a big fight with Peggy, Al finds himself alone with Sherry Cherry, a stunning woman with long, blonde hair who wants to have no-strings sex with Al. As tempted as Al is, he turns her down to the cheers and applause of our audience.

Al then walks into his own house holding a paper bag, out of which he pulls a long, blonde wig (styled just like Sherry's hair) and, says to Peg: "Wear this." Peggy, without saying a word, puts it on and, as Al carries her upstairs to the bedroom, the audience applauds and laughs even louder.

With all the criticism we took over sexual content, Common Sense Media, an influential group advocating on behalf of children for decency in television, cautioned parents about sexuality and rude behavior in *Married... With Children* but also said:

"Parents need to know that this show, which was purposely designed to test the boundaries of network prime-time TV, mines adult themes for laughs; caution is recommended when allowing tweens and young teens to watch. References to sexual behavior (including masturbation) fly fast and furiously, there are crude references to body parts and homosexuality, and characters constantly insult and belittle each other. All of that said, hidden under the insults and tight clothes is a nuclear family that cares about each other." Can I get a "Whoa, Bundy!"

CHAPTER 15

SEASON 9: THE NETWORK GOES PSYCHO OVER "PSYCHO DAD"

"'MARRIED' HONCHO FEUDING WITH FOX"

...READ THE HEADLINE IN *VARIETY*, the closely followed Hollywood show business daily. The article went on to say: "Michael Moye, the producer of *Married... With Children* has refused to write two episodes of his show in protest over a decision by FOX."

Michael, who was running the show by himself again this season, was protesting FOX's refusal to air a two-part episode we shot in Season 8 that featured Al Bundy and his NO MA'AM buddies travelling to Washington, D.C. to stage a protest at a congressional hearing on violence in TV after their favorite show, *Psycho Dad* was taken off the air because the network deemed it too violent.

Moye said that FOX pulled our *Psycho Dad* episodes fearing that the *real* Congress in their real upcoming hearings on violence in TV would retaliate against the network and impose restrictions on their fictional portrayal of violence, as Janet Reno had threatened to do in an announcement that was so eerily close to the premise of our episodes it could easily have been a line out of our script: "If the networks don't significantly reduce television violence," Reno warned, "the White House and Congress will enact laws to do it for you."

When FOX mentioned these hearings in Washington as the basis for not running the *Psycho Dad* shows, Michael said, "I went ballistic and told them, 'You're really concerned that some Senator is going to quote Al Bundy in a congressional debate and sway the mood of an entire nation? Seriously? This is a shoe salesman, guys, and a fictional one, talking about a fictional show to a fictional Congress. I think we really need to calm down.'"

FOX eventually did *calm down* and allowed the episodes to be broadcast but not until a year later, and only after Congress backed off its regulatory threats in favor of the networks promising to create their own guidelines, reminiscent of what happened with the Family Viewing Hour.

"Now that I've had a few decades to cool off," Michael told me, "I can look back on FOX's position and understand that they might've been afraid that our *Psycho Dad* episodes would be viewed as FOX's way of poking fun at the members of Washington's antiviolence coalition…many of whom were probably acquaintances, if not downright buddies, with some of the network higher-ups. If that's the case," Michael added, "then just say so! At least we would've understood better what we had to work with. Instead, we were left to surmise their rationale on our own, and that probably upset us as much as the issue itself."

Though the action of Al actually getting into and addressing a congressional committee represented the broad direction we had been steering the show in lately, the emotional core of the story was classic *Married… With Children*, starting with, Al's attitude about violence on TV:

MARCY: *Psycho Dad* was the most violent program on TV. Did you know that they portrayed an average of eighty-four killings per one-hour show?

AL: Well, a man's gotta reload. And I don't wanna hear all that politically correct rooster poop that television is the cause of all our problems. People don't act a certain way just because it's on TV.

Also touching base with his point of view about marriage:

MARCY: My point, earwig, is that violence on TV desensitizes people.

AL: Well, so does marriage, and they haven't cancelled that yet! Despite all my letters.

And, finally, feeding his long time rivalry with Marcy, who we discover was responsible for the campaign that got *Psycho Dad* cancelled in the first place.

MARCY: Al, violence has no place on the streets or on TV, and we've gotta start somewhere. Today, *Psycho Dad*, tomorrow...everything else that men enjoy.

Though Ed still loved playing the classic Al/Marcy rivalry that kicked off the story in this episode, at this point in the series he thought Amanda herself was starting to push her character in a different, "masculine" direction. "When Marcy was married to Steve." Ed said, "Marcy had been more or less the female in the couple. She was very, very feminine and cute. And then as the show progressed, a change took place where she was the more masculine of the two. She could *grow a tooth*, as we used to say."

Ed was correct that Marcy had gotten a little more *toothy* after she married Jefferson, but as someone who was in the writers' room when those changes were made, I can tell you it had nothing to do with Amanda herself trying to impose *masculinity* on her character. We purposefully wrote Marcy's stepped up, controlling posture as a natural response to her marrying Jefferson who was a more laid-back, less-driven character than Steve, a gigolo if you will, and who she felt needed more direction with his life. We had Jefferson comment on this development too, as when Marcy suggested that Bud and Kelly need a "strong male figure in their lives."

JEFFERSON: What are you gonna do, Marcy, move in? (LAUGHS)

MARCY: What exactly do you mean by that? Do you think I'm bossy? 'Cause I don't think I'm bossy, not bossy at all, Missy! Or are you calling me masculine? 'Cause I'm not masculine, I'm feminine! Now, if you don't want a hook to the liver you'll march on home!!

Marcy especially felt she needed to take the reins with Jefferson in regards to his ambition. Jefferson was written as someone trying to avoid getting a job at all costs but he feels he compensates for that by being a *provider* in other ways.

AL: How does Marcy let you get away with not working?

JEFFERSON: Well, Al, I'll tell ya. Whenever the subject comes up, I just…give her a ride on the ol' Jefferson Airplane. Yep, yep.

So no matter how *bossy* we played Marcy with Jefferson, he was still very attracted to her as was she to him, and hot, passionate sex between them was always on the table, which was more than you could say for Al and Peg.

PEGGY: I want to have sex on the kitchen table.

AL: I want to have a meal on the kitchen table. Learn to live without. I did.

Amanda was supportive of this shift as well. "I'm glad they married Marcy off again," Amanda said. "As a gay person in the entertainment industry where I was cast playing ardently heterosexual women, I would have to fragment a little of my own life. Leave it at the doorstep. At *Married... With Children*, they understood me to be who I was as Amanda, but they also wrote a wonderful character for me to portray. I loved Marcy."

Whatever conflicts that were bubbling under the surface this season, there was much good cheer about the addition of Al's new coworker at the store, Griff, played by Harold Sylvester. There had been several other attempts at pairing Al with a comedic foil at work, which never stuck. The first was talented comic, Ritch Shydner, who debuted in the pilot as Luke, Al's single, carefree, babe-magnet opposite. However, because we were already scoring so strongly with Al and Steve in a very different way, the Al/Luke combo never really worked for us and was soon dropped.

Al's next colleague at the shoe store, Aaron, played by Hill Harper, was a young man who was humbled by Al's legacy of "four touchdowns in one game." Al liked him too and felt obliged to talk Aaron out of marrying his fiancé Angie, the irony being that this reunites Aaron with his old girlfriend, Meg, who is a dead-on African American version of Peg. Aaron was a welcome addition to the show, but Hill Harper's drama career took off and he left to play many other TV series roles, including a recurring one on *CSI: NY.*

In Season 9, Griff replaced Aaron in the shoe store. Griff, like Al, was extremely wary of marriage, but Griff was divorced, giving us a fresh twist whereby Al could get a peek at the other side of the marriage millstone.

> **GRIFF:** I used to have a place to go. Then I got divorced and now I got two places I don't go. She got the house, the car, the money. I got the right to remain silent.

Besides opening up the workplace as an additional setting for stories, Griff was also a welcome addition to the NO MA'AM group and had some featured roles as such. Appearing in forty-three episodes in the final three years of the show, he was one of the most beloved recurring characters in the series.

Harold Sylvester, a veteran African American actor, had some initial misgivings "…about the politics of doing that role, playing that character in this town." However, he came to feel that "…being as silly as you want to be is an affirmation of freedom, and I took that affirmation."

In spite of the show loosening its grip on reality, there were still moments of great comedy this season, especially the two-parter, "Business Sucks: Part 1" and "Business Still Sucks: Part 2." The episode opens on a shot of Al suited up in his football uniform and helmet, charging full speed into a customer's outstretched leg, knocking her over onto the floor in a successful attempt at forcing a size-five shoe onto her size-nine foot. Before

Al can celebrate his *victory*, however, the woman steals his thunder: "See, I told you I was a size five!" and Al, as usual, ends up on the losing end of the encounter.

A beat later, another woman enters the store with a baby in tow and proceeds to breastfeed her infant in front of the two offended guys. Al kicks her out, and tells Griff:

> **AL:** What is happening to this country, when a woman can just waddle into your place of business, your holy sanctuary, and bare her breasts?

This comment would come back to haunt Al, but for now it simply serves as a setup for a physical joke as each of them immediately pull out their own copy of *Big 'Uns* magazine and drool over their respective naked centerfolds. Then, to build on that joke, we reveal that Al is reading a classic *Big 'Uns* and Griff is gazing at a *Black Big 'Uns*. After they steal a furtive glance at each other's centerfolds, without a word of dialogue, they switch magazines and ogle even more lustfully, which gets a huge response from our studio audience.

Though we wrote this particular joke, as we wrote every joke, just to get a big laugh, it turned out to represent much more than that for Harold. "Being in the business from the time I started, in the late '60s early '70s, African American characters never got indulgent stuff like that to do. They left us out of close-ups. So it's important to have a moment like that magazine moment, when you can just be an actor without having any words whatsoever, so people could understand we are more than just political performers."

The next day, as the story heats up, Marcy storms into the store, livid that she heard that Al had banished a woman for breastfeeding and she threatens political action, explaining:

MARCY: Breastfeeding is a natural, biological function!

AL: So is peeing, but you don't see me doing that in public!

MARCY: Well, the last time I looked, the side of my garage was in public.

In Part 2, there is a standoff between a group of Marcy's F.A.N.G. activists, who have occupied the store and are breastfeeding their babies, demanding Al allow them to do so, and Al's counterprotestors from NO MA'AM, who march around the store "topless," showing their flabby girths to make their pigheaded point. Eventually the police show up and rule that breastfeeding is *legal* in the store, but that the topless NO MA'AM goons are guilty of *indecent exposure* and arrested.

This season, Katey was pregnant again and the obvious decision was made to *not* play Peggy as pregnant in the series. The timing of her delivery was such that Peggy was only written completely out of one episode, made short appearances in three others, and was able to appear fully in the remaining twenty-two episodes. Her presence was sorely missed but it also allowed for adding some interesting new characters to freshen up the show, in addition to Griff. One of them was TV reporter Miranda Veracruz de la Jolla Cardinal (Teresa Parente), whose overenunciated, sign-off into the camera: *This is Mi-ran-da Ver-a-cruz de la Joll-a Car-di-nal* becomes a welcome addition to our arsenal of running jokes.

Miranda's TV coverage of events that Al is involved in (especially with NO-MA'AM) is our self-awareness that the show is now so over-the-top, Al's daily activities can constitute "breaking news."

> **MIRANDA:** Hi! This is Miranda Veracruz de la Jolla Cardinal, and we are here live outside the studios of WHBZ, where some sort of proviolence demonstration was supposed to be held. But the only evidence we could find is a crumpled copy of *Penthouse* magazine, and the name Al mysteriously written in the snow.

Another Season 9 episode, "No Pot to Pease In," allowed *Married* to satirize not only itself and FOX, but their old nemesis, Terry Rakolta. When Kelly auditions for a part in a new FOX sitcom, she innocently blabs to the producers about all the craziness of her family. Kelly doesn't get the part but when the show comes on the air we discover that the producers stole her stories and made the real Bundy family, with all their flaws, the basis of their show. This irks all the *real* Bundys except for Al who likes how he is portrayed, but the show is quickly cancelled.

> **MARCY:** Hey guys, have you heard the news? They cancelled *Pease in a Pod*.
>
> **BUD:** What? I thought it was a hit.
>
> **MARCY:** Well, some woman in Michigan didn't like it. She also didn't like football, so that's gone too.

Married... With Children featured a smattering of celebrity guest stars over the years (Vanna White, Terry Bradshaw, Tia

Carrere) but it was far better known as a launching pad for young actors who got some much needed experience and exposure on the controversial show before their careers skyrocketed to a place where, ironically, they would no longer consider appearing on *Married... With Children*. Matt LeBlanc, for example, was in two short-lived *Married... With Children* "spin-offs"—"Vinnie and Bobby" and "Top of the Heap." Three years later, he was cast in *Friends*. Pamela Anderson was featured in an Al Bundy fantasy where he wrestled her and another scantily clad woman in his bed just two years before she became millions of other people's fantasy on *Baywatch*. In Season 9, a wide-eyed, frizzy haired, adorable nineteen-year-old Keri Russell starred as Bud's girlfriend in "Radio Free Trumane" three years before *Felicity* broke her out as the huge multi-series star she is today.

Season 9 would also be the takeoff point for another unknown actress who, at age fifteen, appeared as a non-speaking extra in a scene with Christina and David in the episode "The Undergraduate." Onscreen for just a fleeting moment, you'd have to freeze-frame the tape to recognize her, but this budding artist went on to a career and life filled with such fame and notoriety it would surpass Pamela Anderson, Matt LeBlanc and Keri Russell, appearing in *Beverly Hills, 90210*, *Suits* and, most recently, as a subject of the blockbuster Netflix docuseries *Meghan and Harry*—yes, Meghan Markle.

Though Meghan's fame as perhaps the most controversial member of the royal family ever has far eclipsed her acting career, a screen capture from her 1995 *Married... With Children* debut surfaced recently on *Page 6* of the *New York Post* (go figure) and other tabloid papers, including a feature interview in

Esquire where Meghan recounts her feelings about the show and the better part of the decade she spent behind the scenes of the racy series.

Her father, Thomas Markle, was our director of photography and brought her to the set after school. Meghan recalls, "Every day for ten years, I was on the set of *Married... with Children*, which is a really funny and perverse place for a little girl in a Catholic school uniform to grow up. There were a lot of times my dad would say, 'Meg, why don't you go and help with the craft services [catering] room over there? This is just a little off-color for your eleven-year-old eyes.'"

Meghan remembers she was forbidden from watching the show at home except for the end credits, "so I could give the screen a kiss when I saw my dad's name go by. You gotta think, there were guest stars like Tia Carrere and Traci Lords and Nikki Cox. Those were the kind of women coming in every day. Just picture me with my curly hair and a gap in my teeth and my little school uniform with Keds on, looking up like, 'Hi,' at these very, uh, provocative women. It was a big change from Immaculate Heart Catholic School."

At the height of her enormous popularity, the press was so desperate for any dirt they could dig up on the American Royal, one reporter seriously asked our wardrobe supervisor, Marti Squyres, if "Meghan ever showed up on the set in a princess out-fit?" "Ah, no," Marti wryly replied: "She would show up in her school uniform."

Tom Bower, who wrote the Meghan Markle biography *Revenge*, was more on point when he commented that, due to her experience on *Married* she was, "Introduced into the world of television stars, she loved the glamour. More importantly, she loved the camera. Posing for fun in front of the lens, she became a different person. Conscious of the focus of that glistening glass upon herself, she dreamt, like many young girls in Tinsel town, of her future as a Hollywood star."

Meghan also recalls that the sting of her father banishing her to the craft service table when there was a provocative scene on the stage was counter-balanced by the fact that it was the start of her becoming a foodie. "I spend a lot of my time in craftie," she recalls. "So I can whip up a great snack on a whim with almost nothing."

This year, *Married* was honored with two special retrospective episodes on FOX. One was a celebration of *Married... With Children*'s landmark two hundredth episode. The other was "My Favorite *Married*" where the cast members reveal their favorite episodes, and the audience is treated to highlights from those shows.

The ratings this season continued to decline, but our featured two hundredth episode broadcast, where the unlikely host, haughty author George Plimpton, looked lovingly back at series highlights, lifted us to our highest ratings since the Season 7 premiere.

Another highlight of the season for our *Married... With Children* family came on August 7, 1994, when Katey Sagal gave birth to a baby girl, Sarah Grace White, who has followed in her mother's footsteps and is now a successful actress.

At the end of Season 9, there would be yet another change at the top of the credit roll. Michael decided he no longer wanted to be the sole showrunner, leaving the *Married* hierarchy for the first time without *either* of the original creators of the series and, once again, raising uncertainty among the cast.

"Oftentimes, creative producers won't stay with the show," Amanda Bearse pointed out. "Of course, we missed Ron and Michael and there was nothing like those early years when it was a more blissful experience and we were still sort of in shock that people were watching but I was not of the school that the show could not continue without them. There were other personalities that were on the set that were resistant to that kind of change and because I was so involved as a director on the show, I had a different perspective." And because *I* was chosen as the writer who, for the first time ever, would run the show in Ron and Michael's absence, I would too.

POSTSCRIPT—THE DODGE

When Bruce Wayne drives his sleek, crime-fighting Batmobile through the streets of Gotham, he completes our picture of him as a cool Superhero, just as Magnum, P. I. does when he effortlessly cruises Oahu in a babe-magnet Ferrari. It comes as no surprise, then, when we find a pit-stained Al Bundy chugging through the streets of Chicago in a beat-up old Dodge that belches smoke and breaks down so regularly he often has to push it home. Al's blind allegiance to the Dodge, is a perfect example of how passionate Al is about his choices in life, regardless of how obvious their shortcomings are to others. As when Al boasts:

AL: The Dodge says something about you.

PEGGY: Yeah, it says, "Damn right, I failed."

Or when Al's Dodge was recovered after it had been stolen and he waxes poetic.

> **AL:** I'm glad they found my Dodge 'cause that's my car, and I hate change. It would be like losing one of you guys. Or, Peg, it'd be like trading you in on a brand-new blonde with shiny, factory-warranted hooters. Ah, sure, the first few rides would be nice and everything, but, in the long run…And this, Peg, is what depresses me every day. I realize that…you're the one I want.

> **PEGGY:** Oh, Al.

Besides helping to define Al's character, the Dodge provides so much family history, so many jokes, beats, subplots, and full-blown episodes that it's hard to imagine the series without it. In fact, it's not a stretch to say that, in one way or another, the Dodge was central to almost every milestone in Bundy family history, dating back to Al's defense to his skeptical father for taking a lowly job selling women's shoes to pay for the Dodge. Words that would haunt him forever:

> AL: Oh, Dad. It's just for the summer.

In another episode, we flash back to a scene in high school where the premarital, still sexually active lovebirds are *parked* in the Dodge following the very game where Al scored his legendary four touchdowns. As the high school sweethearts disappear into the backseat to have sex for the fourth time (four touchdowns, anyone?), we hear the first groans of dismay that will soon drown out every bright moment in Al's life, as he tells Peggy that his condom broke.

PEGGY: How could that have happened?

AL: I don't know. It worked before.

PEGGY: You used the same one?!

AL: Hey, they're expensive.

In the blink of an eye, while inside the Dodge, 1) Kelly was accidentally conceived, 2) Al and Peggy go from short-term high school sweethearts to the life sentence that will be their marriage, 3) Al's *part-time* job at the shoe store to pay for the Dodge becomes a *full-time* job to pay for his life, 4) *A high point in Al's life*—scoring four touchdowns in one game—becomes *the* high point in his life against which everything else will always be measured.

To no one's surprise, the rest of the Bundy family hates the Dodge as much as Al loves it, as evidenced by the license plate frame Peggy bought him as a gift that reads: "I'd Rather Be Driving."

In an episode where they think the Dodge is beyond repair and has finally died, Al insists on a proper burial in the backyard. Al becomes so moved as "Amazing Grace" is played during the service that he screams in grief and jumps in the grave. Peggy expresses her grief by shoveling dirt into the open grave that Al has jumped into.

We discover that Kelly, like her mom, has little sympathy for the Dodge as she tells her father that she saw him pushing it home on a sweltering day but ignored him.

AL: Honey, if you saw Dad pushing it, why didn't you come and give me a hand?

KELLY: Well, it looked pretty boring. I mean, you were going so slow and everything. You know a person could get a heart attack pushing a car in this heat.

Bud, who also witnessed his father pushing the car that day and also didn't volunteer to help, wonders why they don't just get a new car, which leads to a rare Bundy teaching moment and restates Al's philosophy about sticking by his choices regardless of how good or bad they were.

AL: Bud, you don't throw something away just because it doesn't work. If that was the case, you wouldn't have a mother.

Though we always used the unreliable Dodge as a metaphor for Al's marriage and to fan the flames of his pathetic life, there is one episode that uses Al's love of the Dodge very differently. In, "Get the Dodge Outta Hell," the entire Bundy clan drives to a car wash where the Dodge somehow gets lost on the lot after being washed and waxed. Al is beside himself in anguish. After a fruitless search of the premises, which includes a classic scene of Al himself being violently washed, waxed, and blown dry as he is drawn through the entire car wash by the pulley chain attached to his foot, the car wash owner has no choice but to offer to buy Al a new car as compensation. Instead of jumping at the deal, as Peggy pleads with him to do, Al insists on making one more attempt to find his precious car.

Al explains to a disconsolate and incredulous Peggy that it's not the Dodge itself he's grieving over, it's something he left inside of it. Peggy scoffs that it's probably a copy of *Big 'Uns Magazine*. Finally, they find the Dodge in the parking lot and the new car offer is immediately off the table. Then, as Peg, Kelly and Bud sadly pile into the Dodge to go home, Al goes to check something in the trunk.

AL: Wait, I gotta see if my stuff's still here.

KELLY: What stuff?

PEGGY: Oh, you know, *Big 'Uns*.

AL: It's not *Big 'Uns*, Peg.

Al opens the trunk, out of the family's view, and reaches for a copy of, sure enough, *Big 'Uns*. He pulls the girlie magazine out, holds it up, and gently removes something from the inside cover. As the camera settles on what he's holding, and we're convinced that Peggy was right, we see that what Al was really saving was a large black-and-white photo of Al, Peggy, Kelly, and Bud all smiling and standing in front of the Bundy home, circa 1987—a Hallmark moment if there ever was one. As the audience reacts in awe to this unexpected, heartfelt moment, it plays without a trace of irony, until text appears across the screen:

For Your Emmy Consideration, Thank You Very Much

The ending, though an unusually touching expression of Al's feelings, also turns out to be a parody, not only of traditional family comedies but of the shameless pandering that TV shows and networks exhibit to be honored for a prestigious, self-congratulatory Hollywood award and its attendant publicity value, for which we were nominated several times but never won...not even for this one.

CHAPTER 16

SEASON 10: GONE BUT NOT FORGOTTEN

WHEN MICHAEL MOYE LEFT THE series this time, he turned the reins over to me and another veteran writer who had worked with Michael extensively and also had a great deal of experience with the show, Kim Weiskopf. Together we would be the first executive producers/showrunners on *Married... With Children* who weren't either Ron or Michael.

With those enormous shoes to fill, Kim and I took comfort in knowing that Michael had agreed to stay on board as a creative consultant for the entire season. This meant he would work with us to break stories and write scripts, which is a big chunk of the job. Whatever continuity and stability Michael provided us early on, however, quickly vanished when the cast returned for production and started balking at the first batch of scripts we had written. Michael made it clear to the actors that he had personally worked on and approved all the scripts, and "nothing had changed," but the cast still felt that the show "wasn't the same."

In a way, I have to admit they were right. The show *wasn't* the same, just like it hadn't been last year or the year before. Nor would it ever be the same again, for a variety of reasons—some avoidable, some not. One way or another, however, we were all still committed to completing the job at hand and we forged ahead to start the new season. It was somewhat akin to being a player on a baseball team that knew it had no chance of making it to the World Series, but was still dedicated to winning as many games as it could and making a name for itself along the way.

On a more positive note, Katey Sagal told us before the season began that she was pregnant again. We were all excited for her and had clearly learned our lesson to *not* make her character pregnant in the show. This year, however, the timing of her pregnancy was such that Katey would have to miss more than fifteen episodes for routine medical demands and precautions, which meant we had to create a storyline for the show to explain why one of *Married*'s favorite characters would be absent from so much screen time.

We decided to fill this gap by bringing Peggy's heretofore only referred to but never seen parents, the Wankers, into the picture. The conceit was that Peggy's mom and dad had split up after many years of marriage and her mom came to Chicago to live with the Bundys. Then, to try and save her parents' failing marriage (and explain Katey's absence), we had Peggy embark on a solo mission to her family's home in Wanker County to track down her runaway father and bring him back into the fold.

Peggy's dad, Ephraim, was played by the incomparable Tim Conway. Her mother was played by the wonderful Kathleen Freeman, whose main *character* attribute, besides hating Al, was that she was so *ginormous* that whenever she lumbered over to the upstairs bathroom or flopped down on her bed, the living room beneath her would shake and plaster would fall down as if it were a major earthquake.

On paper, this all seemed logical and funny. In reality, how-ever, it was a mistake. For years we had been portraying the Wankers (off-screen) as backwoods, drunken, inbred hillbillies—

> **PEGGY:** You know what we say back home in Wanker County?
>
> **AL:** Nothin' spells lovin' like marryin' your cousin."

Or—

> **AL:** Peg, I wonder why you never went after a guy like your father. Or weren't there any chronically unemployed social parasites the month you were in your prime?

We soon discovered that, while these backwoods characters had been funny when pictured in off-camera lines, they ceased to be amusing when the audience actually saw them in person. In retrospect, we should have followed the path they took on *Frasier*, where Niles's wife, Maris, was the butt of many outrageous, off-stage jokes but never appeared on screen in the series. Or, on *Friends*, where Ugly Naked Guy was pictured off-screen by the *Friends* ensemble but his face was never seen by the audience.

"The characters you *never* see," according to legendary sit-com director James Burrows, "provide great foils and allow reactions for their on-screen and real-life counterparts. Characters left to the imagination let the audience work with their mind's eye, and often the vision is better than anything or anyone that can be cast."

Another issue we had to contend with in Season 10 was the cumulative fatigue of having worked for nine years banging out over twenty shows a season on a demanding five-day-a-week production schedule. While it was hard to have too much sympathy for actors who enjoyed tremendous financial and career benefits from a series' long-term success, Ed felt strongly that since they all knew their characters so well, they didn't need the full week to mount a successful show. Given how professional our directors, cast, and crew were, it made some sense, so we agreed to cut rehearsals by one day per week. It was a tough call to make. We figured that the show may suffer slightly from being under-rehearsed but in a long-running series like ours that had other crosses to bear, we had to consider whether we would suffer *more* from not acceding to the stars' demands.

Rehearsal time, however, was only the tip of the iceberg of the problems plaguing Ed O'Neill in the twilight of the show and, to be fair, the other actors had similar legitimate issues as well. First of all, though Ed acknowledged publicly that, "Playing Al Bundy put me on the map," he also said it was, "Like being known for being Porky Pig." I remember once, in the middle of a taping, Ed pulled me aside and told me he didn't want to deliver a familiar, salacious, signature "piggish" joke of Al's. I told him we were as tired of writing them as he was of delivering them but we still had a show to produce and the audience still loved his character and those outrageous lines of his. "Yeah," Ed said through a sigh, "I know." Then, as the director called, "action," Ed magically switched from grumpy Ed O'Neill into pitch-perfect Al Bundy, delivering the line to the audience like the consummate pro he was. Mercifully, he got the laugh I had promised.

Laughs or no laughs, Ed feared he would be forever typecast as Al Bundy. It didn't help that after he was finally got a part in a feature film in a dramatic role, when the audience in a test screening first saw him enter a tense court-martial scene, they burst into laughter and hooted, "Al Bundy!" Ed was cut out of the film and the scene had to be reshot with a different actor.

On another occasion, Ed was driving to meet a producer for a serious role in another film, *State of Grace*, starring Sean Penn. Driving to the interview, Ed was aghast when he saw, on the street across from his meeting, a huge outdoor moving billboard for *Married… With Children* where Peggy held a frying pan that would come down on Al's head, causing his head to shrink into his shirt. Ed did not get the part, though Al Bundy continued to grow in popularity.

To make things worse, people would see Ed in public and make demands that went far beyond a simple autograph. "One woman come up to me in a restaurant," Ed recalled, "and said, 'Hey, I got my girlfriend with me, and it's her birthday. Could you take a picture with her? She likes you. I don't give a fuck about you myself, but she thinks you're, *whatever*.' I said, 'I'll be happy to take a picture, but I want to finish my meal before it gets cold.' She says, 'Well, *we* already ate. What are we supposed to do, hang around for you to finish your meal? You fucking asshole.' This was not the norm," Ed added, "but it happened more than you think."

Years later, having reacted so strongly to incidents like the above, and fans calling him Al and putting their hand down their pants when they saw him on the street, "A switch went on for me," Ed recalls. "Who do you think *they* think you are? They only know you from TV. And I realized, why are you acting like an asshole, this was the greatest job I've ever had? From that minute on, I just went, 'Yeah, okay.' 'So you're Al, right?' 'Yep!'"

Ed would eventually step out of Al Bundy's long shadow and be enormously successful, playing Jay Pritchett in *Modern Family* as well as many other characters. Though Katey, Christina, David, Amanda, and Ted never complained, I could sense they were also weary of playing the same characters with variations of the same jokes.

"I would audition for stuff," Christina Applegate said, "and people would be like, 'Oh my god, she gave the best audition of anyone, but it's *Christina*, and we can't have that name associated with this *masterpiece*.' That happened more times than you can even imagine."

To help shake her "Kelly" image, Christina dyed her signature long, blonde hair red and cut it short for a role she got in the 1997 film, *Nowhere*, though I'm not sure it did too much to shed her role on *Married* as the film was described as "*Beverly Hills, 90210* on acid," and Christina's character name was Dingbat. When Christina returned to *Married* for production at the beginning of Season 10, still sporting her short red hair from the film, we had to plead with her to wear a blonde wig so she would be associated with the Kelly Bundy our audience had come to know and love and, like the trooper she was, she obliged.

All of our actors eventually shed the *Married* image and became very much in demand in other diverse roles, but it was frustrating for them at the time and complicated by the fact that Kim and I had just been awarded custody of the *Married* family, after, as Amanda Bearse put it, "Daddy and Daddy broke up." It was like being a substitute teacher, except everyone knew the real teacher wasn't ever coming back.

Early in Season 10, Buck's trainer, Steven Ritt, approached us with a request that would forever change the course of the series. Buck was slowing down and it was starting to effect his performance on the show and the quality of his waning years so Steve felt it was time for him to quit the show. As difficult as it would be to lose one of our most popular and endearing characters, we knew we had to let him go. In an effort to retain at least a semblance of what Buck represented to the series, however, in the episode where he died, we had him reincarnated during a séance in the Bundy living room into another dog, a cocker spaniel, ironically named Lucky.

As foreign as a séance was to the series, however, we still gave Buck a joke that was steeped in the Bundy tradition. In a scene where Buck has died and finds himself surrounded by heavenly clouds, he asks his guide (Ben Stein) where he is.

THOMAS: You're where animals go when they die.

BUCK: I'm in Oprah's refrigerator?

The biggest disruption in Season 10, however, and the biggest test that Kim and I faced running the show, was that the feud that had been going on *behind the scenes* between Amanda Bearse and Ed O'Neill for years now moved out in *front* of the scenes. Though Ed and Amanda's story was quite dramatic, it's not uncommon on TV shows, especially long-running ones like *Married… With Children*, for the actors to develop strong feelings for each other, that run the gamut from love affairs to hate affairs.

Ashton Kutcher and Mila Kunis fell in love on *That '70s Show* and now live *happily ever after*. On the other hand, things got so bad between comedy stars Penny Marshall and Cindy Williams on the set of their hit show, *Laverne & Shirley*, that even the legendary Garry Marshall, the show's creator and brother of

Penny Marshall, (Laverne), couldn't calm things down. In fact Garry was so upset by the actresses' public behavior on the set, he banned his children from visiting there.

It got to the point on *Married... With Children* where Ed and Amanda argued with each other for long periods of time in front of the other actors, the crew, and anyone who happened to wander in, as they do on a regular basis. It became such a distraction on the stage, cutting into rehearsal time and setting a divisive tone in an otherwise tight unit, that Kim and I felt we had to intervene and scheduled a meeting with the two actors to try to talk it out.

"A lot of it stemmed from the fact that, because I had been directing the show for five seasons," Amanda noted, "I had a different task to perform, and not just as an actor. So that put me in a different place than them."

Ed agreed with her and it seemed to give us some common ground from which to work out a solution, but as they talked, it soon became clear that something much bigger than the *actor-turned-director* issue was fueling this particular fire. Ed eventually confessed that he was especially hurt because Amanda, who had come out as gay in Season 8, was now getting married and had invited everyone else in the cast except for Ed and David Faustino to her wedding.

Amanda was sympathetic, but she had given this a lot of thought and explained to Ed: "I just feel you would find it amusing that me and Becky would come out in matching white tuxedos and walk down the aisle arm in arm and you would be snickering and finding it funny."

"And here's where I went off the rails," Ed told me. "To me, it was like a setup for a joke. Instead of saying—'Well, that's fine, you can invite whoever you want to your wedding.' I said, 'Amanda, what would be *funny* about two girls walking down the aisle of a church with matching white tuxedos on?' Then I started laughing and she said—'See! I told you, you'd think it was funny.' Then, I said, 'Well, you know why I'm laughing, cause it *is* fucking funny and I'm not going to be the only one that doesn't think so. In other words—you may not have been wrong in excluding me.'

"That's where I was completely wrong," Ed said years later, "but I was really hurt and angry that she did not invite me to her wedding. I was trying to just lighten it up. I didn't give a fuck that she was gay. I don't care about sexuality. It really bothered me. I actually said to her, 'You know my brother's gay. And I don't have any problem with my brother. I love my brother. Why would you think that I would have a problem with that?'"

In spite of this distraction and other problems intrinsic to producing a show for that long, we still delivered several episodes in Season 10 that stood out as vintage *Married... With Children*. In "I Can't Believe It's Not Butter," Griff falls madly in love with an especially salacious and graphic phone sex operator he's been calling on a sex hotline, who calls herself "Butter" and he becomes addicted to their sex chats. Al discovers to his horror that Butter is really Peggy's gargantuan mother, who is secretly running a sex phone service out of the Bundy house to pick up money on the side. Al tries to protect Griff from the revelation of this nightmare by having Peggy pass herself off as Butter on the hotline the next time Griff calls and try to reject his advances, but when Griff shows up at the Bundy house and Peggy's mother, in spite of Al and Peggy's best efforts, identifies herself as Butter, Griff is humiliated and horrified and the audience explodes with laughter.

In "The Hood, the Bud, and the Kelly," Al insists that he and his NO MA'AM buddies can save money by installing a satellite TV dish on the roof of his house by themselves. After continuously falling off the roof and crashing to the ground, they finally install the dish. In the process, however, they discover, that in spite of the concussions and broken bones they are suffering, spending time together on the roof, without their wives and kids, gives them total freedom from their everyday lives, and they settle in for an extended stay...bringing lounge chairs, a barbeque, food, and various creature comforts you wouldn't expect to find to this otherwise uninhabitable, stark environment, which they still prefer to their lives down in their houses.

Finally, in Season 10's "Bud Hits the Books," Bud comes home from school and makes a difficult confession to Al that sets up what seems to be a classic sitcom Golden Moment, but instead, turns into a blistering satire of every touching parent/child bonding scene you have ever seen on any other family show.

BUD: I was caught having sex in the school library.

AL: All right! That's my boy!

AL SHAKES BUD'S HAND.

AL: Who's the lucky girl?

BUD: You're shaking her.

AL PULLS AWAY HIS HAND IN DISGUST.
BUD GETS UP.

Compare that exchange to one on *The Cosby Show* when Vanessa comes home from school complaining that kids are picking on her because she is too rich.

> **CLAIR:** Vanessa, you are rich, because you have got a family that loves you!

Al may deep down love Bud as much as Cliff and Clair love Vanessa and he may express it in very nontraditional ways, but his immediate response to Bud's pleas for help is to shut him out and allow him to face the consequences of this humiliating act on his own.

> **BUD:** Dad, I'm gonna be tried by the university deans! I might not be able to graduate! Could you give me a hand?

> **AL:** Obviously, you have too many as it is!

Later in the episode, however, after Al is moved to go support his son at the trial they are holding for his "crime" at the school library after his best buddies admit to having been caught in similar, even worse public masturbatory indiscretions:

> **IKE:** Oh, I give Bud credit. The library is a pretty creative place. Most creative place I ever did it was on an airplane.

> **JEFFERSON:** You did it in the bathroom on an airplane?

IKE: Who said anything about a bathroom?

This leads to Al and NO MA'AM coming to Bud's rescue by marching to the school with placards, passionately chanting:

AL & NO MA'AM: 4-3-2-1 Bud's alone but he has fun! 2-4-6-8 it's his only steady date! 1-2-3-4 He shouldn't have to lock the door!

Al's heartfelt gesture was uncharacteristically moving and paternal, but it ends up, as usual, backfiring. Unbeknownst to Al, the case against Bud at school had already been settled in Bud's favor and the results had been sealed from the public, so, much to Bud's relief, no one else even knew about it. That is, until Al and NO MA'AM arrive with their noisy public protest, followed by the reporter from the local TV station, who shows up and says, into camera, in her signature accentuated style:

MIRANDA: This is Miranda Veracruz de la Jolla Cardinal broadcasting live at Trumaine College, where the group called "NO MA'AM" is here picketing in support of Bud Bundy's inalienable right as an American to touch himself in the library.

As this rocky season ended with a frustrated cast, a continued erosion of the ratings but FOX still renewing the series for Season 11, I decided it was now my turn to leave the show to work on my own projects, as did my co-executive producer, Kim Weiskopf. Michael Moye, who had been a creative consultant this year, also left the show, this time for good, and the studio had to turn to someone who had no history with the show at all to run it.

Amanda Bearse, who directed six episodes in Season 10 and would direct nine more in the next one, was very generous about the leadership of Pamela Eells, the talented, experienced writer/producer who was brought in to run the show for the next year, but Amanda would nonetheless describe Season 11, as, "The year when all hell broke loose." Stay tuned.

POSTSCRIPT—THE LITTLE GUY

Timing can be critical for the fate of any TV series. The *Happy Days* pilot was originally broadcast in 1972 and then summarily rejected for broadcast by ABC. Two years later, however, buoyed by the success of *American Graffiti*, which also starred Ron Howard, the network ordered *Happy Days* to a series, which was then timed perfectly to ride the nostalgia wave of the '70s and become the number-one show on television. The TV series, *M*A*S*H*, though set in the Korean War, was fortuitously timed to capture the anti–Vietnam War sentiment of its era and went on to became one of the most successful shows of all time.

Married... With Children was also well timed. "It stormed into a cathode-lit world of cuddly babied, cocooning yuppies and a beatific Michael J. Fox," wrote TV critic, Rick DuBrow. "In a medium that increasingly wants to teach us little life lessons—look, there's Doogie Howser, M.D., learning about death and getting his first boner!—*Married* revels in frivolity. Nothing is taught, revealed, espoused. No issues are solved."

Timing alone, however, can't fully explain the *Married* phenomenon. After all, there were several other out-of-the-box shows (*Tracey Ullman, Mr. President, 21 Jump Street*) penned by TV writers with even more impressive writing pedigrees (Jim Brooks,

Ed. Weinberger, Stephen J. Cannell), cast with proven star power (Johnny Depp, George C. Scott, Madilyn Kahn) that debuted on FOX at the same time as *Married* but failed to resonate so deeply with the viewing public.

Though we are extremely proud of the humor, the stories, the execution, and the cast of our show, one of the main reasons cited by critics and viewers for *Married... With Children*'s extremely fervent fan base was how Al's unceasing fights about fairness at work, the cost of living, the DMV, network TV, phony advertising, corporate corruption, and so on was a one-to-one stand-in for our audience's struggle against the same soul-crushing forces. What made him even more sympathetic was, as journalist Tom Foster, put it: "Almost every remark he made and action he took, Al paid for. As controversial as the show was, people loved it, and it was balanced in the way it took everything out on the worst offender."

For example, when Al takes a one-man stand against the phone company for a false charge on his bill, he gets his service cut off, his family ends up hating him (even more than usual), and his mother-in-law shows up to visit because she couldn't reach Peggy on their now-dead phone line. Even though Al realizes he's not going to win, however, he is just assuredly not going to quit.

The same holds when Peggy suggests that Al call a roofer to fix the hole in the roof.

> **AL:** Right there, Peg, is the problem with America. We've lost our spirit of self-reliance. Something's leaking, call someone. Something's broken, call someone. One of the kids suffers a ruptured appendix, call someone. Whatever happened to the spirit of "I

can fix it myself"? Whatever happened to rugged, American manhood?

You know for sure that Al is going to fall off the roof the minute he goes up there, but you can't help but enjoy it when, after his initial fall, foolish pride makes him refuse to learn his lesson and he keeps falling to the ground over and over again, as he does later in another episode when he and his buddies try to install a satellite dish.

Anyone who has single-handedly gone up against a bureaucracy can get behind Al's missive to city hall and can't help but gleefully imagining the reaction of the smug jerk who receives it:

> **AL:** Dear maggots and foul bureaucrats. I pay taxes! (ASIDE, TO PEGGY) They'll never check. (CONTINUES READING LETTER) You grafting pigs use my money to wine and dine cheap bimbos, never once thinking to share them with the rest of us. So please fix the pothole in my driveway, and the street light above it…Signed, a voter. (TO PEGGY) They'll never check!

Another very relatable little-guy episode was based on the fallout from the real life 1994 Major League Baseball strike. Al and his NO MA'AM cronies having no sympathy for the super-rich players' salary demands organized their own baseball team (sponsored by the nudie bars), and played against other average-Joe teams (sponsored by competing nudie bars) at now-empty major-league stadiums. They draw crowds and become folk heroes until they also end up going on strike…also for more money. Good-natured guest stars included Major League superstars Mike Piazza, Frank Thomas, Dave Winfield, and Joe Morgan—who were happy to appear on *Married... With Children* even though the show was taking huge swipes at them and their inflated salary demands.

The little-guy episode that struck the biggest chord with our audience, however, was Season 7's "Un-Alful Entry," where Al, awakened by a burglar in the middle of the night, punches the offender's lights out. When the police arrive, Al is hailed as a local hero but before he can enjoy his newfound status, which he plans to cash in on by selling advertising messages sewn on his shirt, he is hauled into court and sued for causing physical and mental damage to the intruder.

Al, who would no sooner hire a lawyer than a roofer, makes his own case, as only he can:

> **AL:** Your Honor, I don't know the law nor do I really know how to pleasure a woman. I have no interest in either. The point is...a man comes into my house...he better be carrying a summons or a pizza. But this man wasn't...so I called in the marines (HOLDS UP ONE FIST)...and the 51st Airborne (HOLDS UP THE OTHER). So in conclusion, Your Honor...if you rule against me...you rule against every man who fought for his country. The boys at San Juan Hill and the boys at Iwo Jima. Audie Murphy, Eddie Murphy, Murphy Brown...the cheap brown shoes that every working-man is proud to use...to kick the heinie of any man who invades his home.

Al is ruled *guilty* by the judge and ordered to pay the $50,000. Adding insult to ignorance, Al says that since he doesn't have the $50,000 anyway, he might as well go for $100,000 and punches the burglar in the face again, assuring the delighted audience that besides being on their side, Al, like his fan base, doesn't have to worry about learning anything from his experience.

CHAPTER 17

SEASON 11: ENDING WITHOUT AN ENDING

FOR THE PAST FEW SEASONS, the Ed-Amanda feud was pretty much contained within walls of the *Married... With Children* sound stage. By Season 11, however, as the expression goes, the walls had ears and the doors had eyes. It was not only playing out in the rehearsal hall, in the press, but, of course, online. Even the most casual observer who took the trouble to Google, *Married... With Children* would be linked to many stories on the subject. Some true...

"Ed O'Neill Reveals Behind-the-Scenes Friction with "Married... With Children" Costar Amanda Bearse."

"Ed O'Neill's Beef with Amanda Bearse"

...some *more* true.

"Amanda Bearse Banned Ed O'Neill from Her Wedding."

Amanda, as always, tried to put it in perspective. "Ten years is a long time for any group of people to spend that sort of constancy together, both in front of and behind the camera." "There were other elements that were there too," she noted, "and perhaps it'll come out in a book someday." Well, *someday* is here and though, to me, it doesn't merit an entire book, any authentic account of the *Married... With Children* story would be incomplete without looking at how this conflict played out in the what would turn out to be the historic series' final year.

"I follow the Thumper rule," Bearse told a crowd at a fan convention in Raleigh, North Carolina, in 2018 when asked about her rocky relationship with O'Neill. "If you don't have something nice to say, don't say anything at all." Though she generally followed her own edict and had many positive things to say about the show and the people attached to it, she also went on to say: "I will share, *he* was not happy towards the end of the series, so that affected everything. The dynamics and the whole regimen of the show shifted. And those who were in a position of power really took advantage of it and it became a very difficult day-to-day process and it didn't have to be. That was the season [11] where if you were a fly on the wall, you would understand." To put it in her terms, if *all* hell hadn't broken loose, at least *some* of it had.

Ed and Amanda, to their credit, spoke very openly in many forums, including the pages of this book, about their versions of what happened in this final season and why. "The truth," as another actor, Steve Coogan, once said, "is somewhere down the middle of funny and serious."

Let's start with the *funny*. Amanda is directing Episode 6 of Season 11, "A Bundy Thanksgiving," her fourth episode out of the nine she would direct this season. It is Thanksgiving morning and Peg explains to Marcy why she won't be cooking her family a turkey.

PEGGY: Huh? You expect me to cook on a holiday? Homemaking is a job too, you know.

Al: Why don't you apply for it, Peg?

Al, however, is nonetheless looking forward to observing an even more cherished Thanksgiving dining tradition that dates back to the fondest memories of his childhood.

AL: Mom would serve Dad the traditional Wild Turkey and then chug the rest of the bottle. We'd weave on down to Aunt Maddie's to buy a sweet potato pie. Then go back home, the folks would pass out, and I'd have me that sweet potato pie all to myself.

Al and Griff thus drive through the countryside to Aunt Maddie's bakery to purchase one of her magical pies. When they arrive, however, they discover that Aunt Maddie had just died and her funeral was about to get under way. Al goes with Griff to the funeral where Al is so stricken with grief—not so much over losing Aunt Maddie, but of *his* Thanksgiving treat—he ends up stealing Aunt Maddie's last pie, which was cradled in her arms, from her open coffin.

Now for the *serious*. In the funeral scene, before Al pries the pie from Aunt Maddie's death grip, Griff joins the pastor and the gospel choir in a rousing, traditional, jazz-influenced funeral dance. "I was watching how Amanda was shooting the dance," Ed recalls. "And she was shooting Harold (Griff) from the waist up. So I went over to Amanda, polite as I could be, and I said— 'You know this is that New Orleans thing, where they'—And she said, 'Yes, I'm aware.' And I said, 'But you're shooting him from the waist up.' And she said, 'That's correct, that's the shot I want.' And I said, 'Don't you think it would be more effective if you shot him full body because the way his hips and his legs are moving, that's a big part of the dance?' And she said—'Why don't you let me worry about the shooting.' And we got into an argument and I said—'Listen, we've got to talk about this because the show is the next day.' And she said—'Fine.' And I said, 'I'll call you tonight at home.'"

"I called her that night," Ed remembers, "and whoever she was with answered the phone and said that she's taking a bath. I said, okay, that's fine, but have her call me back because I need to talk to her, but she never did. The next day, I went to work and I was plenty fucking pissed off. I went into the hair and makeup room where she was getting worked on, and I said—'What is wrong with you? Why didn't you call me back? You said you were going to.' And that went into—'Oh, aren't you the bully. Aren't you the bully.'

"Then I said, 'You know your problem, Amanda, you're not too smart.' And I actually made this comparison where I said—'I've got a button that says, "get rid of Amanda Bearse." You've got one that says, "Get rid of Ed O'Neill." The problem is, *yours* doesn't work. If I press mine, you're gonna be gone.' But I would *never* have done that. I loved the relationship between Marcy and Al. I enjoyed all those scenes we did together. Remember when she did the orgasm, when she lit the cigarette and she closed her eyes and did the little shudder. I showed her how to do that. And that wasn't the only time I did something for her, because I liked her and what I was trying to tell her had nothing to do with *her*, it was all about the *show*."

Years later, Ed retold the "who's got the better button" story in a video interview he was recording for the archives of the American Academy of Television Arts and "I blew the whistle on myself," Ed said, "because that got out to the internet to the gay community, and they said—'This motherfucker's a nasty, fucking mean son of a bitch.' Now, by the way, I could care less what other people think of me. I never have, that's my problem. But I just thought—oh, man, I fucked up. I made a mistake. And I apologized to her for the mistake. It crossed the line but it had nothing to do with her sexuality. Nothing."

When I asked Ed if he felt he was making the same mistake once again by telling me the story for this book, he made no apologies, and added: "You can also say I enjoyed working with Amanda Bearse and that I thought she did a great job on the show. And when you do a show eleven years, you're gonna have some days where you may not be, ah, Emily Post, you know."

"The last season was very difficult," Amanda said. "Ed and I were very good friends when we first started the show. We enjoyed a lot of time working together. By the end of the run of the show, that was not the case. There were confrontations. I'm also a very vocal person," she added. "I'm not passive aggressive, I wouldn't say that I'm aggressive, but I will stand up for myself and I will stand up for other people and, so sometimes in the throes of that, conflict would arise and it's unfortunate because it didn't have to be that way, but it was."

As a side note, if you watch "A Bundy Thanksgiving" closely, you'll note that Amanda ended up shooting the funeral dance in a wide shot to include Griff's gyrating hip and leg moves and that the hours of agony surrounding that moment accounted for only about twenty seconds of air time.

Some have suggested that Ed and Amanda's off-screen hostility actually improved Al and Marcy's on screen performances. Having witnessed the seasons before and during their conflicts,

I feel, however, they were both always so committed to shooting the best show possible that whenever a director called out, "… and action," (even when that director was Amanda Bearse) they became the 100 percent embodiment of Al and Marcy, respectively. For example, in the very Thanksgiving episode where Ed took such strong exception to Amanda's shot choices, Al and Marcy played an earlier scene together where they were sniping at each other in such classic, gleeful enmity it could easily have been from Season 2.

An even bigger testament to their professionalism and their ability to check their personal conflicts at the door, comes in Season 11's "Lez Be Friends." At the end of the episode, as Al tries to convince Marcy to patch up the family feud she's having with her cousin Mandy (who has just come out to her as a lesbian), he shifts so convincingly and seamlessly to empathic BFF that without realizing it, Al and a tearful Marcy find themselves locked in the comfort of each other's arms. Until…

MARCY: Al?

AL: Yeah?

MARCY: Are we alone together in my bedroom, hugging in the middle of the night?

AL: Mm-hmmm.

They pause, then scream at each other to, in effect, reset the relationship.

Season 11 also saw the historic, prime-time run of *Married… With Children* come to an end in much the same way it began— butting heads with FOX. This time the issue wasn't about making PMS jokes, showing side boob, or airing an episode about a violent, albeit fictional show called *Psycho Dad*. *Married* viewers had become so inured to our brand of irreverent humor that FOX wasn't concerned with offending people anymore. This time, the bad blood, as the curtain dropped for the last time on *Married... With Children*, had nothing to do with what we put on the air, but rather, the *how*, the *why* and especially the *when* of the network's decision to finally take us off the air.

While there are thousands of variables in keeping a TV show alive, there is only one constant in killing it—when the network starts continually moving your time slot around, you can be sure you're on life support. In Season 11, FOX moved *Married... With Children* four times in six months. Even *All in The Family*, which was number one in its time slot four years in a row couldn't survive CBS moving it five times in the next four years, especially in a prestreaming era when you could only watch your favorite TV show on the day and time it was scheduled.

When *Married... With Children* debuted in back in 1986, it ran on Sunday night at 8 PM eastern where our ratings were a mere whisper. In 1989, FOX moved us to Sunday at 8:30 PM where we picked up viewers. We stayed at Sunday at 8:30 until 1989, where our numbers kept growing. Then FOX moved us to Sunday at 9 PM where we did very well for a while but eventually started to decline. *Married*, however, was still pulling high enough ratings in the limited FOX universe—especially among the highly coveted young male demographic—that we occupied that space until the spring of 1996. In Season 11, however, our show literally became a moving target...one that, soon, no one could find.

In September we were moved to Saturday at 9 PM eastern. In December we were shuffled to Sunday at 7:30 PM, then, less than one month later, to Monday at 9:30 PM. Only one month after that, we were shifted to Monday night at 9 PM, which would serve as our final resting place. Although there was much anguish among the producers and the cast about the show being bounced around and then cancelled, in the end it was the *timing* of the decision, the *manner* in which it was revealed, and, above all else, the resulting inability to do a farewell show that elicited the biggest outcry.

FOX waited a full six weeks after the end of production to announce our cancellation. This meant, even if FOX had wanted one, it wouldn't have been feasible for us to return to produce a fitting finale—a typically heart-rending, highlight-filled episode that ties up all the loose ends of the characters and bids the audience a fond farewell.

These swan song episodes, almost obligatory in shows with *Married... With Children*'s longevity, are designed to honor the legacy of the show for the audience and to create a cathartic memorial for the cast, crew, and everyone involved in the series. When it was clear we had been cancelled and that no finale was in the offing, fans lit up the internet with protests that they had been cheated out of a farewell show from the series they had been so deeply invested in.

Ed recalls, when he was on stage rehearsing what turned out to be the last episode of the last season: "A bunch of FOX guys showed up and I thought why the fuck are they here? They came to me and they said, 'Is there any way we can make this episode into a possible *last show*, because we're not sure where we are yet and we're going into hiatus.' I said, 'No, it's impossible,' because if we're gonna do a last show it's got to be good. It's got to be well thought out and well written and it's too late to change this episode."

The actors didn't even find out they were cancelled directly from anyone at FOX. Christina Applegate, appearing on the *Jimmy Kimmel Show,* years later, said, "I actually learned we were cancelled from the radio, but not firsthand." A friend of Christina's heard about it while listening to a local morning talk show and told the shocked actress, who had no idea at the time that she was out of a job.

Ed O'Neill, appearing on *The Ellen DeGeneres Show,* recalled that he found out on vacation in his hometown of Youngstown, Ohio, when a car with a "Just Married" sign pulled over and the newlyweds got out and told him how much they loved the show and that they were sorry it was cancelled (they had also heard about it on the radio). Ed was stunned that they knew before he did, but graciously told them, "It was better to hear it from you," and treated them to a bottle of champagne.

"I was at the gym on the Lifecycle bike and I heard it on the TV," Katey Sagal told me. "It was terrible. I remember that summer when Peter Roth took me to lunch to apologize." Peter, who Katey said was the "menschier" of all the different FOX presidents who ran the network under our run, bemoaned the cancellation and went on to say to the press: "It was a brilliantly conceived parody that dared to take a shot at the most beloved forms on television. It was funny, painfully honest, and it defined the FOX philosophy in that it was distinctive, bold, alternative programming that the viewer cannot get anywhere else. Despite

any criticism of it, anyone who really knows the show under-
stands that beyond the mean-spiritedness was a reaffirmation of
family—even if," he added, "it was a different kind of family
than we are used to seeing."

When Ed met with Peter Roth, however, they played out
an entirely different scene than the one that transpired with his
TV wife. After Roth expressed his regrets to Ed about cancelling
the show, Ed told him: "Well that's not bothering me so much
as—no gifts for the cast? Not even a going-away gift? I said, 'You
know I hear they bought the Golden Girls Mercedes Benzes,'
and he said to me, 'Ed, do you think we would let you guys ride
into the sunset without a wonderful gift?' I said, 'OK, but just
a helpful hint—I've already got steak knives.' Roth said—'Oh,
you're funny.' But they never did give us a gift. By the way, I don't
really care about that, I really don't. What I wanted was a last
show. Can you imagine the ratings we would have gotten, if they
advertised it—*Married... With Children*'s last episode?"

As a long-time veteran of the show, I too was disappointed
when I heard about the cancellation but, to be honest, I was not
entirely surprised. There had been a lot of signs recently point-
ing in the direction of the nearest exit—the "time-slot roulette,"
the overall ratings decline, and something very few people were
talking about, at least not publicly, the budget. Though the show
was launched on a minimal budget, by this time everyone's pay-
days, especially the actors, writers, and directors had become
astronomical because the show at its peak had become a huge
profit center. The network was weighing these fixed costs against
the potential upside of a twelfth season of a show that had now
slipped precipitously in the ratings and could not command

the same advertising revenue it had in the past. None of this, to my mind, however, justified FOX *not* allowing us to shoot a series finale.

What did surprise me in looking back at the series, however, was that several episodes in Season 11 were in themselves very fitting "finale-like" tributes to the series. It's almost as if the writers were subconsciously aware that the end was nigh and wanted to wrap things up for the show. Pamela Eells, who was running the show that year, confirmed this: "It is absolutely correct that we kept trying to do a couple of *finale-esque* episodes. I remember the endless tension during that season, especially the last half of it, when Ed and everyone very justifiably wanted the courtesy of being able to put a great period on the end of this groundbreaking show, but FOX refused to do it."

The first example of this "unofficial farewell" is a three-part episode called "Breaking Up is Easy to Do" where, in Part 1, Al and Peggy have the fight of all fights and he moves out to a ramshackle apartment, which is so marginal, you can see, hear, and feel a succession of jet planes landing outside his window at the very adjacent airport. After Al and Peggy's fight escalates to the point where it looks like there's no turning back, they both start to miss each other and we dissolve to *Married*'s send-up of a conventional sappy, sitcom montage of short clips of the tender moments the couple shared over the years. In a traditional show, these images flash through the couples' *memory banks* and make them realize, in spite of what they're going through now, they still belong together and they make up. These were the "motivating, tender moments" in *Married*'s make-up montage.

1. Al uses the phone cord as a noose, trying to hang himself.

2. Peggy uses a toothbrush to scrub Al's sweaty armpits and then employs the same brush to clean his teeth.

3. Al convulses in an "electric chair" when Peggy pulls the switch as part of a TV game show episode where they are contestants.

4. Peggy kicks Al off of the top bunk of the bunk beds they are sleeping in, causing him to smash through the top floor and crash land in the living room.

5. Al rubs Peggy's butt in bed, as she always begs him to do, but, unseen by her, we see that he is wearing a thick, rubber work glove.

These shared *fond* memories and the fact that Peggy puts the icing on the cake by giving Al his very own subscription to *TV Guide* motivate Al to drive Peggy to their old necking spot when things were good—Maple Lane. Al parks the Dodge and puts a move on Peggy, clearly designed to patch things up, and says:

AL: This car is built to last, just like our love.

Which is the cue for the Dodge to immediately drop off its axles and fall apart…a perfect metaphor for the twisted car wreck in which their life is, and forever will be, entangled.

As much as this three-part episode gives a full picture and, also, the suggestion of a resolution to Al and Peg's roller-coaster marriage, the penultimate episode of the season, "How to Marry a Moron," provides a moment that comes as close to a series finale as the show would ever come. At Kelly's wedding, right before the holy vows of matrimony, Al discovers that her fiancé, Lonnie Tot, has not only been cheating on her, but has had other wives that he and his wealthy upper-crust family have been hiding from her. This triggers Al, who stood to enormously benefit financially from the marriage, to give a speech to the Tots and the rest of the wedding party that delivers in a nutshell, or a *buttshell*, as Kelly would say, what the series is all about.

> **AL:** So that's the kind of low-life scum you people are. No respect for the torturous sanctity of marriage. Well, let me tell you something. We Bundys may have our faults, but we believe that marriage should be forever. No matter how pitiful or disgusting it may be to wake up to the same horrifying face each day. That's what the marriage vows are all about. And anyone who can't stand the nagging, bonbon-eating heat should stay out of the whining, sex-starved kitchen.

Lonnie then asks Kelly if she's sure she doesn't still want to be a Tot, and Kelly says with all the sincerity she can muster,

> **KELLY:** I never thought I'd ever say this, but right now I'd rather be a Bundy.

Wouldn't we all?

FADE OUT:

THE END

AFTERWORD

AFTER BECOMING ONE OF THE longest-running, most influential sitcoms in America, *Married... With Children* set its sights on the world...and the world set its sights right back on *Married... With Children*. More than fifty countries ran the original American series, either dubbed or with subtitles. It became so popular abroad that many countries whose cultures were much more morally restrictive than ours, shot their own versions using indigenous actors and adapting the American scripts into their own language. Some even adapted the title: (Russia) *Happy Together*, (Croatia) *The Waters of Marriage*, and (Germany), *Help, My Family Is Crazy*.

These foreign remakes were so popular in Argentina, Chile, and Russia that they each shot over two hundred of the 262 originals. When Russia, where it ran five nights a week, ran out of original scripts to adapt, they wrote and shot 119 new ones, some of which, for the sake of continuity, were written by original series writers, including myself and fellow writer/producer Katherine Green. A statue of the Russian Al Bundy, Gena Bukin, stands in the center of a public square in Yekaterinburg, the fourth-largest city in Russia and home of the Bukins/Bundys in the show.

I was fortunate enough to personally experience how the Bundy ethos translated to a foreign culture when I was selected to go to Tel Aviv to supervise the launch of the Israeli-language version of *Married... With Children*. While I was there, two out of the ten episodes I was supervising were ones I had originally written for the American market. I was amazed and delighted by how closely the originals translated to another culture, but I had another experience that even more persuasively drove the universality of the *Married* humor home to me.

After work almost every night, I found myself alone in a foreign country and, other than a few friends I made on the show, with no one to share a meal or a friendly chat. On one such night, I was sitting alone at the bar of an upscale Israeli restaurant and as I drank wine and ate dinner, I struck up a conversation with my mid-thirties bartender. After regaling me with tales of his adventures in the Israeli Defense Forces, where most young Israeli men and women serve, he asked me what I was doing in Tel Aviv. Knowing I could never match the gravitas of his story, I humbly told him I was working on the Israeli production of *Married... With Children* and, without a blink, in the middle of the crowded restaurant, with all the gusto of a live nightclub performance, he broke into a robust version of the theme song from Al's favorite TV show, *Psycho Dad*:

> *Who's that riding in the sun?*
> *Who's the man with the itchy gun?*
> *Who's the man who kills for fun?*
> *Psycho Dad, Psycho Dad, Psycho Dad.*

Here I was, halfway around the world, in a foreign culture, where I didn't speak the language, at least two decades removed from when I had worked on the show and a total stranger in a crowded restaurant is passionately singing me a song that appeared on our series, at most, three times. I can guarantee

I'm the only person who ever cried to the strains of *Psycho Dad*, but tears welled up in my eyes and pride filled my heart at the cross-cultural happenstance of this moment, which was also living proof of how *Married... With Children* translated to foreign cultures.

Who would have thought that while struggling to survive in the third season of our rebel show, when Marcy Vosburgh advised an offended *Married... With Children* viewer that if she was so affronted she should simply change the channel to another show, that millions of people in America and all over the world would instead change their channel to *Married... With Children*. Creators Ron Leavitt and Michael Moye must have had a gut feeling when, shortly after they fell in love with the name Al Bundy, Ted Bundy became the most notorious serial killer of his time. "And all these people," Ron said, "were gently suggesting that we might want to change the name of our character, lest people associate him with such a horrible murderer."

"Don't worry about it." Michael replied, "people will remember Al Bundy long after Ted Bundy is gone and buried."

ABOUT THE AUTHOR

RICHARD GURMAN HOLDS A BACHELOR's degree in sociology and a master's degree in journalism from the University of California at Berkeley. Richard worked in Hollywood for over thirty-five years writing, producing, and showrunning such popular TV shows as *Happy Days, Laverne & Shirley, Mork & Mindy, Diff'rent Strokes, Facts of Life, Married... With Children,* and *Still Standing.* In 2017, he produced the documentary film *This Is Bob Hope* for the PBS series *American Masters,* and in 2020, along with director John Scheinfeld, he executive produced the documentary *The Happy Days of Garry Marshall* for ABC.